Hunters in the Digital Age

David Wicks

Copyright © 2018 David Wicks

All rights reserved.

ISBN: 1985842327
ISBN-13: 978-1985842328

DEDICATION

To all tech business founders - the true pioneers of our age.

CONTENTS

DEDICATION iii
ACKNOWLEDGEMENTS vii
FOREWORD ix
PREFACE xi

PART I : STORIES 1
   1.   FIGHTING FIRES 2
   2.   STORIES FROM THE FAST 50 7
   3.   MY STORY 69

PART II: THE FOUNDERS' WORLD 79
   1.   A DIFFERENT VIEW 80
   2.   FAILURES 85
   3.   THE MAP OF GROWTH 88

PART III: FINDING YOUR WAY 126
   1.   KEY QUESTIONS TO HELP YOU STEER 127
   2.   LIFT OFF! 137

ABOUT THE AUTHOR 140
DISCLAIMER 141
REFERENCES 142

ACKNOWLEDGEMENTS

I would like to thank Richard Woods, who inspired me to embark on this project and David Cobb and the team at Deloitte for their wonderful support. It has been a real pleasure to meet, talk and collaborate with many fellow winners of the Deloitte UK Technology Fast 50, in particular, James Caddy, Joel Davis, Elnar Hajiyev, Oyvind Henriksen, Colin McLellan, Alexis Prenn, Andy Savage, Jon Slinn, Hiroki Takeuchi, Stephen Upstone and Paul Volkaerts. I would also like to thank the following people who helped me shape my ideas for this book: Karen Stainsby, Marc de Marcillac, Alex Merry, Susan Payton, Ed Bootle, Kevin Emamy and Chris Leeks. Finally, I will be forever indebted to all I have worked alongside and learnt from over the past 26 years.

DAVID WICKS

FOREWORD

For the past twenty years, the Deloitte UK Technology Fast 50 has recognised the achievements of the UK's fastest growing technology companies. The awards are designed to celebrate the success of some of the most exciting and innovative technology companies in the country. The competition gives us fantastic insight into these businesses, all of which have remarkable ultra-rapid growth in common.

The UK technology sector has grown tremendously over the past two decades. New subsectors such as agritech, fintech, medtech, which barely existed in the 1990s, continue to emerge and disrupt the current landscape, and with them come new companies and ideas. We have seen the type of companies entering the Fast 50 change considerably, and have a wider range of entrants than ever before. Companies who have been a part of the programme in previous years, like Deliveroo and Skyscanner, have become household names, recognised for their success worldwide and genuine 'tech unicorns', born and bred in the UK.

This year marks the 21st Deloitte UK Technology Fast 50 awards. As we celebrate this 'coming of age' milestone, and after three years at the helm, I will be handing over the reins to Duncan Down, who will take the awards on to new heights. I am delighted to have had the opportunity to play a part in the Deloitte UK Technology Fast 50, and to witness the recognition of success and value it has generated for swathes of companies within this time. The Fast 50 is a truly unique competition, and demonstrates that the UK tech sector continues to generate fast growing, impressive companies that can compete on a global level.

David Cobb, lead partner of the Deloitte UK Technology Fast 50

DAVID WICKS

PREFACE

This is a book for tech business founders and the leaders and advisors who work alongside them. It is for anyone who aspires to grow an outstanding business and change the world around us.

The UK tech industry flourishes. Following two decades of rapid evolution, digital technologies have truly come of age. Innovation ecosystems with incubators, accelerators, investor and founder networks have spread from Silicon Valley to the UK. All provide many opportunities to build a successful technology business.

Over the past 26 years, I have seen many creative individuals and teams set up businesses. They chase their dreams to make a difference, be the masters of their own destiny, generate wealth and leave a lasting legacy.

Many highly successful UK start-ups that have achieved massive growth are not household names. They transform the world around us with little recognition beyond their niche markets. Their founders are not held up as examples of how to create huge value from nothing and how to make a real difference in the world. Whilst many do not seek this recognition, we need these role models and pathfinders to inspire the next wave of entrepreneurs and thus benefit everyone within the UK economy.

Over the past 20 years, the Deloitte UK Technology Fast 50 has recognised these businesses. This book celebrates a milestone anniversary and the significant contribution winners have made. My hope is that more will follow in their inspirational footsteps.

Many businesses fail due to an inability to stand out from the crowd, to offer something unique and of high value. Those that clear this first hurdle may start to see accelerating revenue growth but then must learn rapidly how to scale their delivery. Networks of successful founders are invaluable but only go so far. Founders know they cannot share all their challenges externally. The key knowledge and experience has to be established within the company.

To mature the business, it is vital not to discard or break important elements that have brought you this far. If you have taken the external investment route, the company will have experienced directors with financial, sales and marketing expertise. They will focus on high growth and do whatever they can to help you achieve this. But do they really understand your values, culture and team? Is their agenda 100% aligned with yours?

You may be a serial entrepreneur who has learnt from previous business mistakes and have many battle scars. But what if you do not have any experience yet? For many, the opportunity to achieve phenomenal business growth comes as a once in a lifetime opportunity. One that you do not want to throw away.

This book draws on the significant experience of successful founders and leaders from some of the fastest growing tech businesses in the UK. Celebrating their success, it illuminates the paths you too can take if you are to follow in their pioneering footsteps. It will help you ask key questions at pivotal times and find the right answers and solutions for you and your business.

Many start their journey, not realising the commitment and personal sacrifice required to succeed. The real achievement is to create sustained growth and a lasting legacy without giving up everything you hold dear in the rest of your life. You might have very understanding family and friends, a 10 year plan and an agreement to put the business first then leave it all behind for a life of wealthy leisure. In the meantime, life happens and you may find yourself missing important milestones as you become a stranger to yourself and those you care about. Hopefully, you will have worked out how to avoid this and achieve some sort of balance. But as your business growth accelerates, this will become more and more challenging. If you do not take the right actions and share the load with a trusted team, the demands of the business will become unbearable.

If you want to build a significant business, your life's work perhaps, and not jump ship early then read this book. It will show you the way to achieve sustained success without sacrificing everything else that is important to you.

Many UK companies have shown incredible early success only to be bought by international giants who operate with different agendas, constraints and cultures. Founders see their pride and joy, built up over many years, rapidly turn to dust. The wealth they generated enables a comfortable lifestyle and the ability to invest and nurture other founders' new businesses. But this will never be the same as the pride they felt in their own company. It will never make up for losing their personal legacy.

If you look to achieve rapid success and wealth through a quick sale of your business, without caring what you leave behind, then this book is not for you. If you want to be proud of your immense achievement and establish a legacy that lasts, *Hunters in the Digital Age* can help you understand what it takes to do this.

The book is divided into 3 sections.

Part I, **Stories**, shares the stories of extraordinarily successful UK businesses as well as my own journey of learning and discovery. Each unique story reveals significant keys to success and can be read in isolation or with the other stories to form a more comprehensive picture, thus helping develop depth of understanding.

Part II, **The Founders' World**, shares the perspectives and world views of successful founders. These are very different to those of the many who have followed the well trodden path of employment in established organisations. Introducing *The Map of Growth*, Part II reveals the key paths to success and the classic traps and minefields to avoid.

Part III, **Finding Your Way**, shows you essential questions to ask and when to ask them so that you can find your own answers and paths towards phenomenal growth and a legacy that endures.

PART I : STORIES

1. FIGHTING FIRES

"They all gone and left you on your own Mr Ross?" asks Dennis, our company cleaner, as he bustles in to the office.

"Yeah. They don't know what hard work is these youngsters." I joke.

Dennis laughs. He knows it's a joke and begins vacuuming up the daily detritus of a busy office. As the drone of Dennis's machine starts to hypnotise me, I reflect on how the business is going and what may lie ahead.

> Yes, everyone here does work hard. Problem is, I'm working hard too but I'm not sure my efforts are going in the right direction. I've got some tough decisions ahead and I don't want to get it wrong.
>
> I love finding solutions. People say I'm deeply driven and passionate about what I'm doing. And I'm a person who pulls out all the stops when it counts. I'm building a great company with a fantastic team of bright, high-energy, committed people.
>
> I want to make a difference. The dream is that one day, we'll be financially successful doing what we all love - creating innovative products. And when I eventually hang my hat up and move on, I'll be leaving a lasting legacy.
>
> And I'm well on the way to doing that. We've got a healthy turnover. Amazing opportunities are appearing and everyone's strapping themselves in for a rapid take-off. But ... and there is a 'but', it's all starting to feel a bit shaky. It's like the wings we've built are starting to show cracks.
>
> The team's overloaded with work and what worries me more is the sales team are selling faster than we can deliver. First class customer service is so important to me. I don't ever want our customers to feel neglected or undervalued but I'm not sure what to do next ...

> *Competitors are out there, biting at our heels like hungry dogs. If we don't keep customers happy, they'll go somewhere else. That would be disastrous!*

"Lift your feet up Mr. Ross" Dennis interjects as he pushes his vacuum under my desk. I dutifully obey and return to my thoughts.

> *Morale in the team used to be so high but it feels like it's sliding. What happens if key team players get disillusioned and leave? They're all special and important but I don't think we could succeed if Rahul or Sylvia walked. They're brilliant and they'd easily get snapped up.*
>
> *Like me, everyone's here because they want to create cutting-edge solutions and services. But we just don't have the time or capacity now to design or build new products. That's why I started this business – so that we could do what we love. I want to be able to grab new opportunities with both hands, but I'm really worried we're not in a strong enough position to take them on.*
>
> *This could be make-or-break time and there's a lot of pressure on me to get it right. I feel responsible for all the people who believe in me and my vision, all those who came on board to help me grow the business to what it is today. I don't want to let them down. I know them, I know their families … I feel so responsible.*

Outside, a fire engine rushes by, sirens blazing, a momentary distraction from my inner tirade.

> *I'm giving 100% of myself to this business (and more). I'm not sure I've got that much more to give. It's definitely taking its toll on me. It's hard to get to sleep these days and when I do, I wake up with it all going round and round in my head. Annie's getting really fed up of me tossing and turning all night. I can't keep disturbing her sleep – she's got her own business to run. We don't seem to be seeing much of each other these days and that's adding to the strain.*

I've put my heart and soul into this venture and we've the potential to be phenomenally successful. All signs are promising and the future looks good ... but I don't know ... I feel pulled in every direction. I'm just not sure what to focus on or how to make sure we've all the right pieces in place. I want to get this right. I don't want to fail myself or the team. I've got to do something soon before the cracks get any bigger and we all fall into the ocean ...

I get up and pour the last of the coffee. I have to think!

I have to focus on growing the team, but it takes so long to recruit and it's hard finding the right people. At this stage of the business, we need more talented, motivated people that already have the essential skills and capabilities. But I'm not quite sure how to do that. No one (especially me) wants to be hand-holding new recruits. Anyone who joins us from now on has got to be a huge asset to the team from day one.

And when we've got them we're going to need more space. Maybe I'll have to split the team up but I really don't want a 'them and us' thing going on! I've heard people talk about 'silos' and I don't want that.

The thing is ... I'm not entirely sure everyone is doing the right job as we move forward. If I have to fire anyone I'm going to be right outside my comfort zone. I know what it's like to lose a job and I don't want to be the one to bring the axe crashing down.

The leadership team's really got to be stronger too but it's difficult to know how I can make that happen. I spend far too much time getting involved in stuff I shouldn't have to ... like the 'people managing' side of it all. That area's just not 'my thing' but someone has to do it. I really didn't realise how much of that sort of stuff there was in running a business and just how much time it would eat up.

And we must start looking at all our procedures and processes. They all worked fine when we were small but I'm not sure they're solid enough to see us through fast growth. We've got to

> be able to adapt as we grow. What worked in the past might not work in the future.

I put down my empty mug, only now realising how stewed and bitter its contents have been.

> *Now Tim and the other investors are on my back. I know they want growth and results. But their expectations are so unrealistic. What happens if they sell out to a competitor?*
>
> *I can't hold off any longer ... I know I need help in so many directions but I'm not sure exactly what I need or who to trust. Should I bring someone in from outside, or would that be a kick in the teeth to my own management team? I'm not sure how I would handle that one.*
>
> *And if I do bring someone in from outside, will they get what we're all about ... our values and vision? I can't see a 'one-size-fits-all' model working here. That wouldn't take into account our unique approach and what we want.*
>
> *I know what I want to achieve, I just don't know how to get there. If I had a magic wand, I would find more highly productive and committed people somehow, to take on the additional work. We'd all share those core values that've made us successful so far, and one clear vision. All the right tools and processes would be in place.*
>
> *There'd be a great culture ... a strong leadership team. One that was built on trust and support. We'd talk honestly to each other and not be afraid to suggest new ideas or talk about our mistakes without feeling a fool. We'd build a loyal customer base who'd rave about us and a healthy balance sheet. That would keep the investors happy!*
>
> *I'd like to think I'd get some respect from my peers, colleagues ... the industry. I'd be able to hold my head up high, feel proud of what we've achieved. Then maybe, one day, I could step back from it all and do other things with my time ... spend time on the bigger picture.*

"You got no home to go to Mr. Ross?" quips Dennis as he jerks me out of my reverie.

"Umm ... yes, if I can remember where home is Dennis!" I laugh at my own joke, but I notice Dennis isn't laughing.

"Go home Mr. Ross ... go home." His voice takes on a caring tone as he packs away his cleaning stuff.

"Thanks Dennis." I reply. "You're right. Maybe it's time I listened to some sound advice."

2. STORIES FROM THE FAST 50

The past 20 years has seen rapid evolution in digital technologies and an extremely fertile environment in which new ventures can exploit them. In 1997, most web sites were no more than digital brochures. Desk top computers were widespread in offices, educational establishments and an increasing number of homes. However, since the birth of the smart phone in 2007, the number of devices in our pockets has grown to 2.3 billion in a world of 7.6 billion people. Consumers have experienced a huge shift from the world wide web to new social media channels and communities; from mass media scheduled on TV and Radio to niche content streamed on demand.

This revolution has been enabled by the rise of ubiquitous services on cloud computing platforms and ever expanding wireless networks. The consumer can now be entertained and informed whenever and wherever they wish. Not only that, but the era of mass customisation and personalisation has finally begun after two centuries in a world of mass production. With awesome computing power, Artificial Intelligence and machine learning algorithms have come of age to mine gigantic mountains of data created by new devices and online platforms. The next wave of transformation may soon be upon us if the blockchain fulfils its expectations, with distributed ledgers, smart contracts and a trust system without intermediaries.

We are fortunate to be living in the most exciting revolutionary age of human kind thus far. The following stories are windows into the entrepreneurial world that has driven this change. These founders have harnessed and evolved emerging technologies to create new products and services that transform our world. They have achieved staggering growth rates over 4-5 year periods of between x5 and x1000. Often, successful businesses are in the right place at the right time. But this is not due to blind luck. Their founders have chosen a domain, hunted down opportunities, focussed their resources, changed direction when needed and delivered solutions rapidly to an exponentially increasing number of customers. They truly are 'Hunters in the Digital Age'.

Each has started from a different point and taken a particular path. They have explored and learnt along the way, recognising that there is no right and wrong - just what works and what doesn't. Here, I present the themes and variations that have led to their success: their vision, values, culture, focus, speed, learning, evolution, talent, team, leadership, products, customers and finally their dramatic sustained growth. My aim is to show how you can follow these examples and become a successful hunter, grow your own business to these levels and create a lasting legacy.

The following accounts are excerpts from interviews with founders and leaders who have won the Deloitte UK Technology Fast 50 award. These stories illustrate the range and extremes of entrepreneur from the exceptionally bright young change maker who questions the validity of old concepts and pushes the boundaries, to the mature entrepreneur who has experienced many problems for themselves and can now see how new technology can address them.

Hiroki Takeuchi, Founder and CEO, GoCardless
Combining years of financial services experience with a customer-driven approach, GoCardless is transforming online payments and the direct debit industry. As a next generation payments company, it makes it incredibly cheap and easy for anyone to take payments online using the Direct Debit infrastructure. In 2017, GoCardless was awarded 8th place in the Fast 50 with 2097% growth.

> "I think that for me, the journey of GoCardless has really been one of discovery. It's not a case of us having seen the problem that we're solving right now from the outset. It was more something that we discovered as we started to build a business for the first time."

Hiroki began his entrepreneurial journey studying Mathematics at Oxford University where he joined the Entrepreneurs' Society and learnt about the Silicon Valley culture. He quickly identified an opportunity to address group payments for club events where existing methods were cumbersome.

> "Going into this, we didn't know anything about payments, so we were really coming at it with fresh eyes."

At the time, the vast majority of payments online were being done by credit or debit card. These were far from ideal for group payments. Hiroki and his fellow founders realised that Direct Debit was far better suited but much harder to access and use. The opportunity was to build technology on top of the back end direct debit mechanisms, open up access to them and make them much easier to use.

The founders were awarded a place in the Silicon Valley technology incubator, Y Combinator. Moving to San Francisco, they learnt from the very deep level of expertise of program partners and tech founders such as Mark Zuckerberg, Brian Chesky and Drew Houston.

As they built their first product on top of PayPal, they quickly developed significant knowledge of payment systems. However, projected growth did not follow the classic 'hockey stick' curve. At the culmination of the program, whilst presenting to a room full of the top Silicon Valley investors on Demo Day, they realised they had to rethink their approach and returned to London.

Despite this, they had made significant progress on the backend, getting access to banking relationships and regulatory approvals, learning how the payments market and direct debit systems worked.

The first breakthrough came from a meeting with Dwayne Jackson, the founder of the online accounting software, Kashflow, which had 20,000 customers. Dwayne understood their exciting vision and financed the integration between the two solutions. This brought about an important step change as customers adopted the GoCardless solution. With the integration funding they began building their team.

> "I think that massively important, is the cultural fit. I think in those early days, you're forming what is going to be the basis of the culture of your company. We were very deliberate and quite hesitant on those first hires, in terms of making sure that we hired the right people from a culture perspective. We took a relatively slow approach there with the belief that bad hires from a cultural perspective early on could really set us off on the wrong track."

> "One of the great things about the Y Combinator program was that the brand around it was very strong, especially within the development community. We were able to attract very like-minded people through that connection. That really helped a lot."

Fast forward to 2018 and the GoCardless team has now over 200 people with 80 working in product development. The organisation has been through several iterations.

> "The things that work when you're four people don't work when there're ten. Those things don't work when you're 30 etc., etc. At each stage of the company's scale, we have to revisit the way that we approach things and the way that we organise ourselves. Absolutely, there certainly have been many iterations."

Finding the right talent to do this was far from easy.

> "Hiring is the biggest challenge. Engineers in particular were always massively in demand. There's a huge amount of growth in the technology sector, especially in London. That competition is pretty fierce. I think that that's always been one of the big blockers, has been the hiring."

Another breakthrough happened once experienced leadership came on board.

> "We'd been a 20-25 person product development organisation for a while and we managed to really massively increase that last year. There was a huge acceleration when we got the right leadership in place. I think that hiring and leadership are the two aspects that are really key."

As the team expanded, conscious, structured communication from the leadership became increasingly important if organisational silos were to be avoided.

> "This is one of those things that is an ongoing battle. I wouldn't say that we've cracked it. The organisation that you work with when you were smaller doesn't scale and you have to revisit it.

I think it's the same when it comes to communication. That's absolutely key. Everything from the way that we run our debriefs, all company meetings, the way that various functions communicate with each other. There's no silver bullet to that. I wish there was, but there isn't. It's really about getting down into the details and fixing the problems as they arise."

Opening a second office in Paris took these challenges to the next level.

"Obviously, that's quite a big step change in the sense that you have to change the way you think about communication. Everything from having to record or stream the meetings that we have to various offices, being a lot better at how we store information so that it's not just accessible because you were there to hear it, but it's accessible after the fact."

A clear understanding of the company values and evolving culture was required.

"I don't think that you can control culture. I think that the culture is a manifestation of everyone's behaviours . As you go into different markets and different countries, each country has its own specific culture. I don't think it's the right thing to do, to force your culture onto others. I think it's more about having an alignment of the values, and being very clear about what you believe and what you care about. As long as you have alignment on those, then the culture can adapt around it, but still be fundamentally compatible."

Now operating in France, Germany, and Spain, the vision is to do this globally whilst maintaining focus.

"A big part of our vision, and what we're building right now is building out that product capability to really have that global network so that you can collect from anywhere to anywhere in any currency. That's really a big part of what we're building. A big part of the product development team's efforts is going into that now."

"I think at a more fundamental level, we have this belief that these bank-to-bank systems, like direct debit, are a better way of

> collecting recurring payments. We have strong belief that if we focus on that, then there's a huge market that we can go and address and help. Having conviction in that belief, but also at the same time being responsive to those differences across markets. That's a balancing act that we have to walk the line of."

Today, the GoCardless journey continues. Hiroki understands that there will be continued twists and turns as they navigate towards sustained and growing success.

> "I have a very strong belief that even the best-laid plans never end up working out the way that you imagine. It's not like there's a straight line between start and success. It's much more of a zigzag. The importance of action over having the absolute best decision. The importance of iterating through mistakes. That's probably one of the macro things I've definitely learnt."

His advice to aspiring founders is clear.

> "It's a long journey, but an incredibly rewarding one. I think that it's definitely one of the most rewarding things I've done in my life so far. I consider the journey still at the very early stages. I think it's a great thing to get into, but one of the things I'd say is, 'Be very conscious about the magnitude of the journey you're getting into'.
>
> I see a lot of people who think they want to start businesses, but when they realise what is actually involved in the journey of starting a business, they maybe rethink things. I think it's about going in with your eyes open."

> **Paul Volkaerts, CEO and Founder, Nervecentre Software**
> Founded in 2010, Nervecentre Software has won the Fast 50 award for three consecutive years (2015-2017), coming 6th in 2016 with growth of 2,702%. This innovative business is a pioneer in bringing clinical applications to mobile technology within acute hospitals of the National Health Service (NHS). It has revolutionised patient safety and productivity whilst making it easier for clinicians to communicate and leverage whole hospital resources. Nervecentre have delivered award-winning mobile solutions to over 30 NHS Trusts in the UK and some of the largest hospitals in Europe.

Paul founded Nervecentre after 10 years as a software developer for a Telecoms company and another 10 years working in sales roles for Cisco. With significant experience of writing and selling software, and deep understanding of the collaboration technologies required by the NHS, he saw the opportunities for mobile solutions in acute healthcare.

He also realised that no one was addressing that market, predominantly because it was hard to deconstruct the requirements and was technically challenging. Decision-making in the NHS is highly skilled and individual. Communication and support of decisions is difficult. Paul was aware of widespread issues with slow decision-making and how this impacted the level of care the hospital was able to provide, especially at night time. Deeply technical, Paul was drawn towards industries that have a strong ethical backing to them. With the NHS he felt he really could make a difference.

Paul was not an entrepreneur in what he calls the 'classic sense'. He did not produce a business plan, seek funding and then hire a team to deliver the plan. Instead, with the right software skills and knowledge of the domain, he believed he could personally create something exceptionally valuable with very little external costs. He invested £5,000 to fund the business for 12 months, by which time he would either be generating revenue or looking for another job.

He met his contacts in hospital IT departments, explored their problems and wrote software to solve them. He saw that no one was really considering the use of mobile technologies in health care. This led him to create the 'Hospital at Night' mobile solution, which quickly brought the right doctor to the right place during the night.

The first six months were very enjoyable and felt stress-free. Paul was relieved to be out of big business with the freedom to do whatever he wanted. After six months, the pressure he put on himself to succeed grew. Stress began to hit hard.

It wasn't until half way through the twelfth month that Paul won his first contract.

> "I remember getting the call to say that I'd won that first contract, and just literally jumping in the air and punching the air, being so excited about that. And that delivered about £250,000 of revenue in that last month of the first year, from £5,000 put into the business, plus my own skill."

Reflecting on his first year, Paul believes being a lone founder was easier for him.

> "Taking all the pressure on yourself feels like a lot, but it's nothing compared to the pressure of letting somebody else down. That's higher pressure than letting yourself down ... I never wanted to be in that position where there was two or three founders, and I was worrying about the financial situation of other people as well."

Paul delivered the projects successfully and hired two people, a nurse with deep domain knowledge and a developer to take on the extra work. For the next few years, Nervecentre doubled revenue and headcount, year upon year.

> "I don't think you know whether you can build a team of people unless you've built a team of people. So it's quite a frightening thing to do."

> "Interviewing someone that you're going to pay their salary out of effectively your personal money, and going from a first year of having no cost to hiring people on fairly reasonable salaries, you know, 50, 60k kind of salaries ... it feels very different than working in a big company and going through a process of interviewing somebody."

> "And at some point during the journey of building a company, you hire people that are wrong, and it's then that you realise if that'd been my first hire, we would have gone bankrupt, because it's so important to get those people right."

Paul put the right people in the right place, proving his strong team building skills and ability to assess an individual's strengths and weaknesses.

For the first few years, he saw the key to success as understanding his customers and building good products. Then, whilst preparing a blog he elicited feedback from a few customers to understand why they bought from Nervecentre.

> "I spoke to a few customers ... 'Why did you choose to work with us?' fully expecting them to say, 'Because your product's really good.' and they didn't. They said, 'Because your people are really good'."

Asking the question 'How can mobile transform health care?', Paul continued to hunt for new problems and propose new solutions.

> "The customer wants to tell you the problem that they're having. What you want to get to is a solution to that problem, and that solution may not have been considered before. So you can't really expect the customer to make the leap from their problem to a solution that is based on what you do and the glue between those two things."

He relied heavily on his own highly skilled team to steer product direction.

> "Skilled nurses ... that fully understand that environment are good not only in engaging with (hospital) Trusts and understanding them, but they're good at keeping the technical ideas under rein. We'll quite often have conversations where we propose a technical solution to a problem and they'll go, 'No. That just won't work. It isn't right. You're focussed on the wrong issue. This is the problem we need to fix'."

Paul is clear on the reason for Nervecentre's success and its phenomenal growth.

> "There's an element of timing and luck. I don't mean luck in the 'lucky' sense of the word, really, because I do think you make your own timing and luck. You end up being in the right place at the right time, but you're in the right place at the right time because you're listening to people, and you're absorbing the environment you're in."

Rather than focus on point products, Paul has developed a collection of related solutions under the umbrella of mobile collaboration.

> "We were able to build software module on top of software module on top of software module, while staying within the philosophy of the business. It helps you, because it helps your customer to understand you."

> "By keeping the philosophy broad, we were able to take people on a journey with us. What that meant is most of the people that bought the first module, bought the second module, bought the third module, because it kind of felt like it was a natural progression."

> "But we were really good, I think, at adapting to the changing needs. Health care needs change on an extremely regular basis, more or less every two years I would say. The whole industry reinvents what is the most important thing for that industry. At the moment, it's probably 'flow'. Two years ago, it was 'paperless'. Two years before that it was 'patient safety'. And in two years' time, who knows what it'll be again?"

He has created a high trust culture led by the management team.

> "In our management meetings, we very much have an open trusted environment. We've all got to the place that we've got to by learning through the process of building the organisation. We've all seen each other's mistakes. We'll all call each other's mistakes out. We'll have open debates as to whose fault something was, without worrying about being at fault."

Nervecentre's success is underpinned by a clear set of values and culture that supports long-term customer relationships.

> "Making people feel part of the company, I think, is about having a culture that people buy into so that they don't feel the need for it to being reinforced all the time. And keeping that culture steady."

> "I find that culture is either reinforced or broken by every decision you make."

> "The first time you put your revenue or your profit ahead of customer success, your culture of doing it like that isn't genuine anymore and people see through it. If you make all of those decisions from that basis, then actually, keeping people together is easier."

Nervecentre remains self-funded, in part due to the strong desire to always put the customer first.

> "I've always feared that investment might split loyalties between the requirement to serve your shareholders, and the requirement to serve your customers. Of course, it doesn't have to. I'm not suggesting it has to. But I've never been certain enough that I had the skill to manage that so that it wasn't detrimental. So it's always been a safer choice for me to say, 'No. I'm just going to keep my one master. My master is my customer. If I only have the one master I know I'm going to serve them well. If I split it and have two, I'm not sure that I could manage that well.' "

With a strong momentum, each time it scales, Nervecentre embraces new challenges.

> "The bigger we get, the bigger problems we can fix. So whereas we used to be focussed on small problems, we now find ourselves of a size, we can fix whole hospital challenges. We've got the team behind us to support 24/7, the largest hospitals in the country relying on us. We've got that skill across the business to be able to support that, to be able to deliver it, and therefore, the same philosophy we had at the start around addressing those challenges. We just feel able to take that to a bigger level."

"We operate at such pace. We're very, very agile, and very fast-moving, which is difficult to do and difficult to maintain, but also difficult to stop. And so, you move at a certain pace to achieve certain things, and when you achieve them you're already running at that pace. And it's difficult then to go, 'Well, we've achieved that, we may as well have a rest for a year'. It's kind of difficult to know how to do that.

Just by its very nature, your ambitions take on a life of their own. You spend a year or 18 months working flat out to try and get the business to be able to deliver some new capability or to enter some new space, and then you do that and you succeed and you've got the momentum, you just want to go with it, really. And, you know, it's not like the NHS is short of problems that technology can help with. There are many, many areas. We've only scratched the surface, really, on what can be achieved with technology and helping to improve quality and/or efficiency. We'll keep going till we run out of steam."

James Caddy, Founding CEO, Orbis Technology
Creating online sports betting, Orbis Technology supplied and customised licensed solutions to all major UK bookmakers together with leaders in other regulated territories, including Macau and Ireland. Acquired by NDS (News Corp) in 2000 for £45M, Orbis went on to grow revenue by 999%, winning the Fast 50 award for two consecutive years. With sustained growth over 10 years, the business was sold to Vitruvian in 2011 for £208M.

Orbis was founded in 1996 when websites were mostly just brochure-wear. The idea that a web page might change depending on data that was held at the back end was relatively new. Orbis provided web application development services, through a product from the United States on an exclusive distributor basis and sold add-on services. It built an impressive list of customers including Telewest, Virgin Mobile, The Times and Mirror Group newspapers. These included applications to present sporting information and betting odds.

The business could have continued supplying generic services, but given the limited resources of a bootstrapped company, it chose to focus on the overwhelming success of its betting applications. Retaining the IPR for these applications, it built a transactional back end, licensed it and OpenBet was born. A unique solution, it attracted most of the UK bookmakers eager to add e-commerce to their traditional betting shops. It also lead to the creation of SkyBet.

Customers paid for an initial perpetual right to use licence and support contract, followed by additional customisations. This enabled Orbis to generate and sustain real profit throughout the whole internet boom.

Led by James Caddy, a strong founding team steered the business towards phenomenal growth, creating and nurturing an extremely creative, talented and performant team.

> "That was deliberate. It wasn't part of some cunning plan. It was deliberate in the sense that I just like people, specifically intelligent, dynamic people. Sometimes opinionated, difficult people actually, I quite like. And there are a lot of those in Orbis."

> "Claire, my wife, said, 'It's like you've got another family' in that I would sometimes get on a train whenever somebody was having a crisis moment and go out and see them. Because it was a big family really. We invested a lot in making a good place to work, and I think we lost five people in the first six years of the company, of their own accord."

> "I think it was a key success factor...I think we achieve the most when we work together. I hope that was one of the things that atmosphere engendered within people. It was a team effort ... I used to have to throw people out of the office at 11pm at night, order them to go home ... I remember those days very fondly. It was all hands to the pump, and we were doing something exciting. It was exciting times."

One of the key early hires was Chris Hall, who designed OpenBet and became CTO. He was described as 'the grain of sand around which we grew the pearl'. This CEO/CTO partnership was pivotal to success.

> *"He was invariably considerably more clever than anybody that X,Y,Z big consultancy was putting in front of you. But he had a great way with him. He didn't butt heads in a way that perhaps some other people might have done. He would just demonstrate without a shadow of a doubt that he was right. That was one of his great strengths, actually. I would always take Chris on a sales call... that's one of the differentiators we had in that core leadership team. We had someone like Chris, who was as good a software developer as you'll ever encounter but with a real grasp of the real world and what customers want and the ability to get on with customers.*
>
> *Incredibly bright young people that we hired saw Chris as an inspiration to them. He was brilliant at that. He should be a teacher. I could understand technical stuff and sale; Chris could as well. That was a real strength, to have your lead technical person getting into human factors, as well as your lead sales commercial person getting the technical side of it. That is one of the things I think we were very lucky to have."*

The team built close relationships with all customers at multiple levels from the leadership to the project teams, delivering new features on a regular basis.

In December 2000, the business was acquired by NDS Limited which provided the financial support and earnout targets that triggered tremendous growth. In just one year, revenues grew from £3.5M to £11.5M.

> *"It was an amazingly good year. The year after wasn't too bad either and that was because we were able to go and get a huge new office, which we hadn't got the covernance to do when we*

were bootstrapping. Which meant we could hire more people, which meant we could make more investments. The market was also going great as well. A lot of things came together. But because we had been acquired we had more money to invest in growth and we delivered profit against that almost immediately. Which is unheard of today. So it was a great year."

"We were delivering significant profit, far more than other business units ... They ultimately sold the company profitably as well. I think it was a good acquisition for NDS. It was good for us as well.

It would be very easy for me to look back and say I never should have sold it, but actually we probably wouldn't have grown. It would have exhausted everyone. You can only bootstrap and get mindshare from people for so long. It has to be set against an objective."

Jon Slinn, Founding CEO, Rockshore
Rockshore, a specialist provider of real-time operational intelligence, focussed on the aviation, rail and telecoms markets. Customers used the accurate up to date operational information to improve their decision-making, simplify processes and collaborate more effectively. Rockshore won the Deloitte award in 2012, generating significant interest in the business and in 2015 was acquired by CACI.

Jon's childhood dream had always been to create and run his own business. He started his career in the mobile phone industry with 3mobile and Nortel, witnessing the build-up of 3G technology and mobile apps. At that time, mobile businesses focussed on hardware and infrastructure , where billions of pounds were invested. Few were really interested in the new apps and services, or could see the revenue potential. Jon took the opportunity to specialise in applications and services as part of a bid team.

When he joined Bitfone, a Californian startup, Jon learnt how to communicate powerful ideas to secure contracts with major businesses. When Bitfone was acquired by HP, he left to start his own company with his brother, Mike, who had just returned from travelling.

The initial product idea came from personal frustration with predicting bus arrival times at local stops. He knew that the data existed in backend systems but was not being made available to people waiting to catch a bus. He asked:

> "Why can't I just SMS a short code number for that bus stop, and get a real-time list of when the buses were arriving, so I don't have to stand in the rain and the cold for 20 minutes. I can set off exactly at the right time."

Jon took this concept forward, to bus companies and Transport for London. Realising that contracts had already been awarded to major contractors (although not due to complete for 5 years), he pivoted to the airline industry and explored opportunities with both Jet2 and easyJet.

The real breakthrough came when the founders approached National Air Traffic Services (NATS) to sell real-time information and provide a client-sized service to consumers such as taxi companies.

> "The concept was right, and I actually phoned up National Air Traffic Services and said, 'We need your data.' They said, 'We can't give you this, and we've been asked before.' They'd been asked by other people who wanted to do similar things, or something related to the data flowing through their systems ... I said, 'That's fascinating. Why not?' They said, 'Because our systems aren't capable of providing it in a way that anybody seems to be able to consume it.' So I said, 'Okay, well let's come and talk to you about that'."

Presenting the story of how they could introduce a solution at the front-end of the legacy servers, Rockshore secured a contract for a proof of concept. A developer they knew was offered a stake in the business to build it. Completing the first version within a few months using a server in his kitchen, he quickly hired a small team and found an office. The work expanded into a complete new platform for collaborative decision-making, part of a European-wide initiative which led to more work in Amsterdam, Rome and Finland.

Separately, Jon was approached by Vodafone to create a device management platform for business users which led to work for BT and AT&T. Within five years, Rockshore had two major legs to its business.

The first development team, originally set up in Sheffield, soon found the local talent pool too small and moved to Leeds, a neighbouring city with a flourishing technical hub. As the founders wanted a team based in the UK, offshoring was never seriously considered. The first developer became CTO but over time the founders realised it was essential that someone led the deliveries rather than provide a pure technical focus. In a parting of the ways, Rockshore appointed a project manager to a general management role.

> *"We always had a big challenge with the technical leadership and vision. The problem with development teams, is they very rapidly work out that you're not a hardcore developer, and they have no respect for you. There's something about software development guys that I think in some respects, it's the modern-day equivalent of the shop floor, and they have a tough attitude towards people that are from outside their world, even if you are supposedly their boss. It doesn't really wash for much. Yes, it was always difficult, and finding the right person that they respected and who could interface with the management team, I think, is one of the hardest roles going. I think it's why, when you see people senior, highly technical people in leadership roles in these big businesses, they're usually the lynchpin of the operation just because of that.*

You get a few that can cross over the line, and very few can. There's very few developers I've seen who actually understand the stresses and strains around the business side of it, and the interface with the customer, and there's very few management people who are able to gain the respect of the development team from a software point of view. We never found the perfect person. We found some great people ... a couple of great developers who stepped up into a head of development type role, but then we'd lose them, because the market was red hot."

"Leeds is a base of businesses around the service industry, especially in brokerage and banking ... you're talking about FTSE 100 businesses with massive firepower, hunting around for talent. And here's a small software business that's kind of giving people a break, and once they've been given a break and given a year or two, they can go to an interview and say, 'Oh yes, I'm involved in leading a team of six or seven, and we're developing real-time software.', they're gone. So we suffered from both of those things. It's hard to find the people, and when you find them, you lose them."

Despite all the challenges of building and retaining a strong software development team in an incredibly competitive region, Rockshore found a way through.

"I don't know whether people know it or not, but the real power of a business is the fact that it is the sum of the parts, but it can survive the loss of any one part. The creation of the joint stock company, the very creation of that as an entity, I always found the most fascinating feat of human engineering. I think it's amazing, because I didn't realise the power and the strength of it, and you can be dynamic and you can start something, but it actually creates a momentum that is all of its own. You lose somebody left, you lose somebody right ... so long as there's enough people pushing it forward, it will go forward.

So that's how we survived, because in any given time period, if you look at the start and the end of four years, we've probably lost 80% of the people in there. Some people will say, ... we shouldn't be losing 80% of people. At the same time we're employing very young people on less money, because we're a start-up and we're trying to bootstrap and create profit, and they're going out for a lot more money to big businesses who are prepared to pay those numbers, and have got the kind of franchise that allows them to pay those numbers. And yet, we still move forward. So we just take the next wave in, and we try and keep some of the talent as long as we can. And we had key people stick around for 4, 5 years' time, and that's a long time really nowadays."

Whilst demonstrating immense commitment and perseverance, the business continued to grow, navigating through challenging deliveries.

"We had some really difficult deliveries to customers. It's really hard at times. And you hear of some of these software projects just going completely off the rails, especially some of the major government ones, and you can get in a really bad place with them. Everybody's scared, nobody thinks you'll ever be right again, everybody thinks it's terminal. Those are the dangerous moments, because you've got to give people belief that there's going to be a way out. 'It's going to be okay, Let's go and make a cup of tea and I'm sure when we come back it'll be alright', kind of thing. So we bootstrapped the business, we had everything to lose. We never didn't deliver. We delivered late on things, but we never didn't deliver, and I'm proud of that. I'm proud of the fact that we just kept going."

With this ethos, Rockshore retained many of its key customers.

"To this day Rockshore, or what is now a division of CACI, supplies National Air Traffic Services, still sell to Vodafone, we still sell to Rome Airport, and these are businesses that we broke into as a team of 5, 6 people. And here we are, over a decade later, and

we're still selling software to them."

This enabled the business to achieve high growth and led to a place in the Deloitte UK Technology Fast 50, 2012. Significant interest was generated worldwide.

> *"What it did do was unleash a tsunami of private equity and VC people. So I went from thinking, 'Maybe one day we'll maybe do something about having some investment in the business because we bootstrapped it completely, and maybe I'll put a slide deck together and go and see what we can do with the next step of the business', to being inundated with phone calls from people saying 'Can I invest in your business?' That was strange. I mean, they were calling up from Boston and New York and California and all over Europe, it was just a tsunami."*

Rockshore was acquired by CACI in 2015. The services continue today leaving Jon with a legacy he is rightly proud of.

> *"I always wanted to build my own business, ever since I was very small, washing cars and delivering papers and wanting to build a business. Rockshore's a proper organisation that from about 7 or 8 years in, anybody else could've taken my role and the business would've carried on. It was a very viable business that was profit-making, employed a good chunk of people. I'm proud of it."*

> **Alexis Prenn, CEO and Founder, Receipt Bank**
> Founded in 2010, Receipt Bank has revolutionised accounting for small business and in 2017 was awarded 7th place in the Fast 50 with 2,947% growth. The first to automate the collection and data extraction from receipts and invoices, Receipt Bank now provide AI and automation technologies focussed on cost savings, effortless bookkeeping and real-time accounting. These solutions are used by over 6,000 accounting and bookkeeping firms as well as 100,000 small business customers globally.

Receipt Bank started as an expenses management business. Founders, Alexis Prenn and Michael Wood, envisaged a need for people to process their reimbursable or small business expenses.

> *"Our previous business had been involved in tax efficient investments, EIS, business proxy relief, venture capital trusts. We had sold quite a lot of these products to high net worth individuals through their accountants. We rang up all these accountants and said, 'Gosh, we've got this terrific, wonderful idea for dealing with all those ghastly bits of paper that your small business clients dump on your desks and expect you to handle. Wouldn't you like us to process them for you?'"*

> *"They all said, 'That's great, but we want you to take care of the invoices, the credit notes, and genuinely all of the costs. Our clients, the small businesses, are happy to raise their sales invoices. It's the cost of the business they don't really like dealing with. Guess what? We don't really like dealing with them either. If you could take care of that, that would be great'. For three weeks, we said, 'No, no, no, you don't understand. We have a strategy. We have a plan. We have a strategy that we are going to be in expenses management.' At the end of three weeks, we said, 'Oh well, stuff it. If that's what they want, we better give it to them.' That was the moment that we, by accident, fell into something called 'bookkeeping productivity'."*

Receipt Bank had found a new market with no competition.

> "Removing filing, removing storage, removing data entry, removing opening envelopes, scanning things, all of that kind of stuff just disappeared. Suddenly, bookkeepers could be infinitely more productive. They could do things much, much more quickly than they were previously doing. Suddenly, there was an opportunity for the information that the client was providing to their bookkeeper to be useful to the client and not just simply for a VAT return. It's a journey we had been on for seven years now. We definitely haven't reached to the end of the journey, where that information, that data, can suddenly be relevant for the owner in terms of where their business is. More and more today, it's ... about using that productivity to make things go faster. When things go faster, the value of the data that's being speeded up becomes more real-time and more useful."

Alexis and Michael explored many features and developed these with an existing team in Bulgaria, progressively moving engineers across to the new work.

> "We created a category. There was no right answer, and it was pretty much, why don't we try a bit of spaghetti and just see whether that will fly. People seemed to like it, so we did a bit more of it. In fact, I would say that probably six years on, what we had was one product, which basically was a collection of all the worst ideas, all the best ideas, we'd ever had. We weren't very good at weeding them out.

> Over the course of the last year or so, we've tried to be much more professional, much more selective in the capabilities that we actively support, develop, enhance, improve, and those that perhaps weren't a good idea when they were originally done. They still aren't a good idea, so maybe we should actually remove them and save everybody the bother."

With customers focussed on their problems, the founders took full responsibility for continuous product innovation.

> "It wasn't obvious to us why our customers should be thinking as deeply about what we were doing as we were. We were the ones who were invested in this. We were the ones who were thinking about these problems. They were approaching it from an inconvenience perspective, which is valid. Of course it's valid, but in terms of Michael and I, we were thinking about this, and we still do think about it 24 hours a day, seven days a week ... constantly. The idea that your customers, with the best will in the world, thinking anything like as deeply about what you're trying to achieve or indeed have a concept as to where you're trying to get to, there's no reason why they should.
>
> I hope, over the course of the years that customers who have been with us a time, can be confident that we will continue to innovate, that they can rely on us for innovation, for original thinking. Some of it may be brilliant. Some of it may be flawed, but in terms of a platform for them to build their business on, confident that we will reinvest both our money and our technology and our thinking into how to make their businesses better, how to make their staff productivity better, more enjoyable, and crucially, of course, how to make their client experience distinctive and original."

Driven by its founders' obsession with continuous improvement, Receipt Bank's approach to innovation has created a world class business information solution.

> "Now, genuinely, we are running, we think, a world class data extraction capability of our own development. We think that that's a core competence. We think that it will commoditise over time, but we think we're going to be the ones that are going to be leading that particular charge.

I think that we definitely, in my mind, separate out the building of the software, the building of the framework, the building of one brick on top of another, from the genuine innovation. Genuine innovation could be around the use and deployment of technologies or how they might be thoughtfully reconfigured to be useful. I think it's the usefulness that is perhaps, for me, in many ways the most exciting thing.

We do have the traditional disciplines around research and product management, but often you're in the business of an incremental improvement rather than necessarily a reimagining."

"I do think there's a difference between founders and professionals. Founders think about this all the time, all the time, and just the volume of iteration, a Rubik's Cube if you like, 'Maybe we could try this. Have we thought about that, or maybe we should try the other? What if we turned it around the other way and turned it on it's head and painted it blue? Maybe that would be better. If we strip that out' ... endless, endless possibilities."

This has been achieved with a vision or North Star to focus only on new ideas that add value.

"While our processes are relatively unstructured, it is helpful to have a clear idea as to where you're actually going. The point I was making about the customers is they have no idea where we're going. Even if we articulate where we're going, they don't necessarily listen to it or believe it.

I think in the terminology people talk about a North Star or whatever, but if you define yourself on basically saving your customers time, any idea, any innovation ... if it doesn't save them time, then it isn't worth looking at. If it saves them lots of time, it's definitely worth looking at."

> *"Say 'No' regularly. It forces you to make choices. Saying 'Yes' commits you to spending time that you don't have and money that you don't have."*

Having started as a bootstrapped business, Receipt Bank hired mainly graduates for its UK team.

> *"We couldn't hire experienced people. We had to hire people who were straight out of university. We justified this on the basis that there were basically two strategies. There was the Real Madrid Galactico strategy where you just simply take lots of money and you go and hire yourself a Galactico or three. Then there was the Glyndebourne Opera strategy. Basically, Glyndebourne is a small opera house, and you don't need to have singers with big names and big voices, and indeed big salaries. You could just go for talented people who were appropriate for the circumstances."*

Guided by their fundamental value of taking personal responsibility, the founders took a different and flexible approach to the organisation and talent development.

> *"One of the things that we stumbled across ... was that the idea that they didn't have a job; they had a role. They had a role document, a role description that basically identified the things for which they were responsible. One of the things that we did was that we tried to allocate how much time was anticipated for each element of their role.*
>
> *Because in a startup roles change very rapidly, we did reviews every three months. We tried to track how the time was changing so that maybe one account manager was now spending all their time doing customer service. That tried to give us an idea roughly where resources were flowing. It was also an interesting thing because there was no point in sitting down to have a performance review about sales if he was spending all his time doing customer service."*

"So performance issues get dealt with as and when, but we need to keep an eye on what you're actually doing with your time. We got into the habit of doing this every three months. We got into the habit also of these were young people on a journey, a career journey, ... a development journey, a journey that recognises their contribution, that recognises the skills that they've acquired, and recognises their value.

The other element around that is personal responsibility... I simply do not understand why an employee expects me, the employer, to be responsible for them. I have no idea. If they're not interested in themselves, why the hell should I be interested?"

"The member of staff wrote their reviews. They lead their reviews. It's their role. It's their career. They do the talking, not the person to whom they report. We're trying to encourage the whole organisation to appreciate personal development, personal responsibility, and these are things that cannot be devolved to the employer."

With a growing team, continuous communication became essential.

"One of the interesting things about communication is that ... the leadership have to repeat endlessly until they are bored rigid. I do mean bored rigid, because you just repeat endlessly. I do think that it is tempting to always look for the shiny and new. When it comes to communication, to recognise that your audience is changing and that if you take for granted that everybody is starting in the same place, they're just simply not. We have to be tolerant of repetition. We have to be tolerant of people who are new who aren't as experienced."

Receipt Bank solutions are transforming their clients' businesses and the world of accountancy.

"When it comes to a business, any business for that matter, what have you got? You've got revenues. They're up, down, sideways. Cost of sales, up, down, sideways. Overheads up, down, sideways. Profit/loss, up, down, sideways. That's it. That's basically it.

Surely as we move to a situation where you've got real-time data, real-time bank information, real-time recording of liability in terms of your invoices, the real-time or estimating of when bills get paid, etc., it should be possible to do genuinely things that say, 'Alexis, if you'd like to make a bit more money, how much more would you like?'

I hope that's ultimately the direction that the accounting industry is going to go. I'm sure that we're passionate believers in accountants and the services they provide to their clients. I think it's an exciting time to be in that world because things that just historically have never been possible, suddenly are. Suddenly, it is genuinely possible to be an advisor. Suddenly, it's possible to use technology to help you to be an advisor."

Colin McLellan, CFO Skyscanner
Winning a place in the Fast 50 for a record seven consecutive years (2009-2015), Skyscanner were acquired in 2016 by Ctrip for £1.4 billion. With self-built technology, six successful acquisitions of smaller companies and global reach, Skyscanner ensures that each month over 60 million travellers worldwide find the best flights, hotels and car hire.

Skyscanner started in 2003, when its founders realised they needed to build a solution that found the cheapest flights for their holiday breaks. It expanded from there with the vision to be useful for people worldwide. Growing flight search from European low cost carriers to scheduled carriers, it then went global, searching hundreds of different airlines across hundreds of thousands of routes.

The Skyscanner product strategy was deliberate and iterative.

> "Whatever you think your product should be, get it out in front of real users as quickly as you can. Get that feedback loop as tight as you can and iterate on it, as quickly as you can. That's the key. Any business that has an idea of a perfect product and goes into dark room for six months to build it, and comes out with, 'Ta-da! Here's our perfect product'. It's not going to be. Because did you ever actually test what customers really wanted and is your execution of what you thought users wanted accurate? Get up front with your users as quick as you can, test it as quickly as you can."

Skyscanner built their own solutions, enhancing these with a series of acquisitions which provided access to world leading technologies and the teams that created them. A recognition that travel is inherently social, led to the acquisition of the social media business, Twizoo, adding a community communication platform to the existing service.

The success of each acquisition has arisen from clarity in both intention and expectation.

> "Once the acquisition's done on the very first day, the people that have been in that business that are acquired feel part of the Skyscanner family and they are very clear of what the objectives are and how we're going to measure it as we go. I think that is really important."

The relatively small size of the acquisitions also helped.

> "It makes it a little bit more straight forward to communicate that purpose and agree the metrics that you're going to be looking at that define success, when the teams are slightly smaller."

But cultural alignment and a shared vision have been the most important factors.

> "All these businesses that we've acquired still had the founders in place, when we acquired them, they still very much had their own culture. What we liked about them, apart from the technology, was there was a lot of alignment about putting the traveller first, and the relationship, about seeing the massive opportunity that online travel continues to represent to take that friction out of the process for people. There's a lot of alignment and collective vision in the culture within the businesses we've acquired."

Skyscanner now have 11 offices globally, with a total team of around 1,000 people, half of whom are outside the original base of Edinburgh. Central to its culture is its North Star to put the traveller first which aligns the whole team and guides everything the business undertakes.

However, hiring has been a significant challenge.

> "Hiring is always a challenge for us because we have more opportunities than we have people to work on them, and deliver them, which is a great place to be. A lot of market places out there … but one of the factors that limits our ability to execute against those opportunities, is being able to hire world class people, particularly software engineers."

> "Skills you're using just now as a software engineer, shouldn't be the same skills that you're using in 18 months or 2 years' time. You need to constantly learn and retrain."

Customer retention has been key to Skyscanner's success.

> "In the early days it was all about repeat visitors, it was all about organic growth, and search engine optimisation. Businesses that think they have to go out and raise 20 million dollars to blow on paid advertising, it's a dangerous place to be. The next year if you haven't captured a way to retain those users, next year you're going to have to spend 20 million dollars just to stand still, not even

> to grow. It's a really dangerous place to be. You need to start to hone your retention of users before you start to spend significant amounts of marketing cash, I would say."

60-70 million people visit Skyscanner's websites and apps, every month. As a meta search site, it is not legally responsible for the tickets. However, Skyscanner still ensures that travellers who transact via its platform, are looked after by the suppliers they buy from. Customer feedback is listened to very carefully.

> "I think fundamentally, travel has been broken for many, many years. It still is in a lot of ways. Even if you know where you want to go, searching and booking your travel arrangements can be quite the stressful experience. The fear of missing out on a cheaper price, the fear that whoever you book with might not be reputable and if they do disappear, can you get your money back? All these kinds of things. It's a very stressful process and Skyscanner fundamentally realises that. We know that trust is at the core of any relationship, but particularly so online, and particularly so in travel.
>
> And by putting the traveller first, and having that trust at front of mind, I think that differentiates us."

Skyscanner, was the first global tech-travel business to integrate with Facebook and Amazon and have used AI technologies to further improve the traveller experience.

> "If somebody were to type in a search within Facebook, 'Find cheapest flights to Paris', for example, then, the Facebook Skyscanner AI bot will respond initially to that query with 'When do you want to travel? How many people do you want to travel with, etc.', to clarify the query. Then, we will do a search and respond with the top 10 best results for that search.
>
> It makes it easier because people are already on that platform, it

means you can do searches within that platform without having to go to the Skyscanner app, or go to the website on the browser and do the search within the search panel. We can do it in a more natural way."

Skyscanner invested and expanded into China, gaining significant knowledge of this market.

"There's a rate of change in China, particularly in Shanghai and Shen Zen. The rate of development and change there is startling, really startling.

China, in a lot of ways, they're leapfrogging the legacy technology that in the West, we've probably become complacent with. And payments is a really good example of that. In Western markets, we've been used to credit cards, we've been used to debit cards. We've had them for 20 years and redeemed them online. In China, they've never really had that concept. And so, when you've grown up using your mobile phone for everything, why would you not use your mobile phone for payments too?

That's the way China works. WeChat is one of the biggest social platforms there, has payments integrated into it. It's connected to your bank account. You've walked in a restaurant but you're like, 'I'm here with a friend', you split the bill on WeChat. You pay your electricity bill via WeChat. That's second nature in China, they don't have that legacy concept of debit cards and credit cards.

Payments is just one example. I'm sure there'll be many more in the years to come, where China's thinking leapfrogs the legacy of what we've been used to in the West."

Skyscanner's growth has been phenomenal. It was acquired by Ctrip in 2016, combining complementary services to take its international expansion further.

> "From Skyscanner's point of view, because of the fortuitous position that we've been in, a very fast growing business, a very profitable business, we didn't really have to do it for the cash, for the funding. There were a lot of options open to us, but for us it was back to putting the traveller first."

> "Our product, just now is flights, hotel, and car hire, but it's very global, whereas Ctrip's dominance really is in China and less so globally. So, when you marry those two things, Skyscanner's global position, we know how to move into new markets, we know how to localise the product properly. Ctrip has that depth of product offering, when you put the two things together, it's going to be really powerful."

Andy Savage, CTO, Paddle
Paddle provide a checkout, eCommerce, marketing and analytics platform to developers and software businesses, allowing them to spend time doing what they love - building incredible products. In 2017 It was awarded 6th place in the Fast 50 with 3,239% growth.

Paddle positions itself as an ecosystem for software platforms.

> "If you've ever built a product and gone out into the market and tried to sell it, you'll quickly realise that you need at least a checkout solution. You're going to need taxes. You're going to need to support your customers. You will probably need analytics to measure all these things. If you're building software, licensing, some explorations, time trials around that. You have to build all these things and these are huge distractions when you could actually be focussing on your core product. If you start building out these things yourself you suddenly find half of your roadmap isn't your product anymore. It's about building all these ancillary services around you."

Paddle provides this efficiently and effectively on a large scale, sharing real insights such as pricing across all customers.

> "We want to have really sincere relationships with our customers. Their success is also our success, and we can offer advice because it helps both of us, and we're in a position to have all this information."

Originally, the plan was to build a marketplace to sell products using dashboards that managed all aspects of the system. However, Paddle found that customers were much more interested in the system that took payments and managed their money. Some started to develop around this platform so they could use it without the marketplace. It became obvious where the value was and the vision clarified. Paddle pivoted and the business grew.

> "Our vision, if you want to be selling a product, is that Paddle is the default way that you go and do that, and that's when I realised we could go from being big to massive. We wanted to position ourselves as the AWS of software tools."

This new direction disrupted the incumbents.

> "I think it's a genuinely good mission, because these are real problems that haven't been solved. There are some incumbents and they move particularly slowly. We've been quite good at taking existing companies business away from them just because they haven't evolved their product in five years. And that's quite typical all over the payments ecosystem."

To move quickly, the team avoided over-engineering and focussed on finding high value sweet spots.

> "It's quite common for an early stage startup to be scrappy and pre-series A. We definitely did that. You do what you've got to do to

> get to the next stage. Unfortunately, you pay for that later. Some of our architecture design from the engineering perspective, can be a bit monolithic in places. But if we'd not done that, we wouldn't be where we are today.
>
> In the early days, not just from an architecture design, I think we probably weren't as iterative as we could have been. 'This is what we think the customer wants. Let's push out this big product and wow them' as opposed to 'Let's put out something small, see if this is what they want and iterate on it and keep going'. If you do it that way you tend to get there quicker, more efficiently, and you actually get a better product. But I think at the time we did what we had to be doing with a less experienced team, and it still got us to where we needed to be."

Since Paddle found the high value product, it has begun re-engineering for sustained high growth.

> "Going forward we're trying to structure things properly. We would try to structure things in a way where they can scale and we can integrate them much more quickly in the future."

Growing the technical team has been a major challenge.

> "Hiring has been the bane of my life and I suspect that is quite common as well. People are the lifeblood of your business and hiring good people is extremely difficult.
>
> We have definitely made many, many mistakes on the hiring front. I think we're in a good place now. We have started to build a dedicated team of people that really care about the individuals they're hiring.
>
> We now have an idea of what is the Paddle culture. I think that's evolving as we go. We have an idea of what we're looking for.

> *We're getting better at assessing that. It's not just some numbers that you want to fill. It's 'I want to get the best people'."*

The need to find and sometimes wait for the best people, is a lesson Paddle learnt the hard way.

> *"Just get the team right. If you get it wrong you will cripple your business. If it takes you X number of months longer than you thought you would to find the right hire, you're going to earn those months back. It might not seem like it at the time. You may seem like you're way off your roadmap because you haven't got the resources to do it. If you hire the wrong person, you're going to be going backwards not forwards. And if you hire the right person they're going to catch up those months and then some more."*

As the team grew, leadership focussed increasingly on structured communication to ensure alignment, avoid silos and to share product knowledge across the sales team.

> *"Communication is a challenge at all levels. If we look at engineering specifically, we have ... a lot of siloed products. We've gone for the model of product centric teams, so that each team will have a product manager, a degree of engineers and QAs and DevOps. Everything to work on their part of the platform. But it does mean that a lot of the knowledge stays within that team, which is potentially dangerous.*
>
> *You need systems in place for having teams talk to the other teams, to learn across the platform. We do what we call 'lunchtime learning', which is where they talk about interesting problems that they've had. We do 'showcase', which is where they showcase to the whole company, all of the things they've been working on. The technical knowledge can be siloed within engineering and that's generally fine. But in terms of what they're working on, the things that they're working towards, we don't want that to just be*

engineering and product. We want that to be across the whole company. These guys on this side of the office are going to have to sell that eventually, and they need to know what it is that we're making, when things are coming and how they're going to do that."

Communication is much more than a tool for Paddle. It is a key part of their culture and is particularly important internally.

"Communication, is one of our company values ... we're really communicative. We do a monthly all-hands. We'll go through exactly the sales figures that we've done. We want to be completely transparent. If the company's going great, we want to tell people it's going great and if it's going bad we want to be saying 'Look guys this is going bad and this is something that we want to fix.' Fortunately, because of our trajectory it tends to be more of the good news than the bad news, but I think we don't want to hide anything from anybody and I think that's really important."

Transparency with customers is also key to strong relationships.

"We have great relationships with our customers. Paddle becomes your solution. You're effectively asking a company to rip out the heart of (or a good chunk of) how they do their business and replace it with us. We know that's probably better for them in the long term, but for some people that's quite a stretch. One of the ways we get around that is having these sincere relationships with them. We can talk about how they're selling their product and we can offer them advice and can say 'Okay well look, we can't drop names but this is what other people have done. Here's the stats, here's how it was successful for them.' For Black Friday and Christmas we can advise 'if you discount by this percent, here is the uplift that other people typically see.' "

During periods of peak consumption, Paddle have significantly matured their operations and resilience.

> "Black Friday is not quite all hands on deck but we keep all the engineers here just in case. We stagger throughout the day and there's big dashboards all around the office. We have dashboards in engineering anyway but on Black Friday they're just everywhere to make sure. We aim for it to be a complete non-event in terms of engineering. This year it was completely smooth. We do a lot of simulations in the run up to Black Friday based on calculations of what we think the load is going to be and then quite a lot more.
>
> We all sailed through fine this year, which is a stark contrast, I'll be honest. If we go back several years ago, even when we did have a degree of elasticity, systems don't necessarily just magically scale horizontally. If you look back at our old monolith, there were some interesting issues at the time."

A high place in the Deloitte UK Technology Fast 50 has already made a significant difference to a business that is still growing its brand.

> "We don't have, necessarily, that strong a brand yet, outside of the sphere we work in, so hiring talent is particularly difficult. So events like this help lift that exposure. And again, the same with commercial relationships. It gives you a validation - a real genuine company rather than a fledgling startup. If you're particularly going after enterprise businesses, they want to know, 'Look guys, if we switch our entire system to you are you going to be around in a year?'. We're like ... 'Yes. Look at how much we've grown'."

Andy is clear about the huge commitment required to deliver success and high sustained growth.

> "Make sure that you have really bought into what you are doing, because this isn't a little job to do. This is going to be your life for the next 10 years, and it's going to be your life all day, every day. So you have to be really passionate about the problem that you are trying to solve, absolutely."

Paddle has learnt the hard way to focus on building products over and above securing additional finance.

> *"Don't focus too much on raising money. Focus on building the products, and the money will come. We actually got really close to signing with someone else who then pulled out on the signing day. So we had invested three full months into that and then had to go and repeat that, and that's like a job on top of your other job already, and it's a huge, huge, huge distraction. I think there's a lot of press and stories, how you have to raise the money to be successful, and that's not necessarily true. You raise it when it's right for you. Don't raise it for the sake of raising it."*

Perhaps the most important lesson has been the development of a strong sense of perspective.

> *"Just realise that whilst you've got all these problems, pretty much everybody else is going through exactly the same problems. If you go into any start-up or a full-grown business, whilst it looks like everything's fine on the outside, I generally think most people inside are just putting out fires left, right, and centre. We've all got these issues that we're trying to overcome. And don't think that because you've got all these problems that that's necessarily indicative of your success, or lack of."*

> **Elnar Hajiyev, Founder and CTO, Realeyes**
> Using webcams and the latest advancements in machine learning technology, Realeyes emotional intelligence tech platform measures how people feel when they watch video content online. It enables brands, agencies and media companies to optimise their video content and target ads to the right audiences. In 2017, after growing its revenue 932% over four years, Realeyes was awarded a prestigious place in the Fast 50. Customers include iconic brands such as Mars, Hershey's and Coca-Cola, agencies including Ipsos, MarketCast and Publicis, and media companies such as Turner, Teads and Oath.

The original vision, developed by Elnar Hajiyev and Mihkel Jäätma whilst studying at Oxford University, was to help companies build a better visual design of any kind. This mainly involved testing websites as well as videos, with a tool that used third party hardware to track accurately the direction of a person's gaze.

By providing the tool in public spaces, they ran a number of trial projects with selected customers. They invited members of the public to quick tests in order to understand how they interacted with the content. A significant need for understanding how people interact with any kind of creative content was discovered. These trials quickly developed into a revenue generating enterprise.

Operational and scaling challenges using the initial approach led to a significant pivot towards more scalable online solutions that did not require third party hardware. Also, whilst it was both valuable and interesting for companies to see what people were looking at, it was even more valuable to understand *why* they were looking at it. When focusing on certain areas did they feel frustrated, happy or just bored?

Generating huge interest from a wide range of customers, Realeyes explored and navigated a course through many opportunities.

> *"When you are exploring, and you're trying to see what works in the market, at the early stages of the company all the way until today, you do have many requests coming to you - from your existing customers that are very happy with you and want to do more business with you, from new customers that want to become your customers, from other companies that perhaps want to explore new opportunities. You're bombarded with all sorts of requests – 'Could you do that, could you add this feature, and could we use your technology in this way?'. It is very hard to manage these requests and to resist the temptation of side tracking and going into yet another adventure, and another adventure. We'd been doing that for quite some time in the beginning of the company. I think if we recognised the importance of the focus early on, we could have potentially progressed a lot faster."*

Realeyes decided it was more important to focus on being very good at measuring emotions, rather than developing gaze tracking in parallel. The business transformed to measure changing facial expressions and other behavioral cues that indicated both the reaction and the levels of audience engagement.

> *"When we were pivoting from gaze tracking to emotion tracking, obviously we had all these customers that we have served for years. Big brand names that we have served for a long time on the gaze tracking technology. We made the decision to pivot to emotions, but they were still coming back to us and asking us to do some more work for them. It was really hard to resist that temptation because it was actually bringing real revenue to the company. It was easy and straight forward, but all of that was eating up the time from the new direction, which we recognised as strategically important."*

The founders witnessed the dawn of Digital video with more video content going online.

> "We saw the trajectory happening in that it's moving from a traditional TV to online, to digital. These days, big brands are generating huge amounts of video content, much more than it would be on traditional TV platforms. This drove us to pivot towards digital video content primarily."

From the start, solutions were developed in the cloud and the product evolved through various exploratory phases and on to growth.

> "We decided to be fully cloud based from day one. At the time, Amazon was only just setting out, so we were one of the first users of Amazon. Now we're fully on Amazon, using many of its services that have evolved over the years. So that definitely helped us in keeping up with the pace, and with the growth of the company. Having said that, it's still very challenging. Just by virtue of being in the cloud doesn't mean that you don't have any scalability issues in the product."

> "I know the challenges that many startups that develop a product face. Certainly one of them is when you're exploring the market, and what kind of features the market needs, and you want to integrate quickly, then you don't spend that much time investing into a very well designed and very well scalable solution because you might be wasting your time. What if nobody needs it or there's not enough traction for that kind of product in the market? You aim to cut corners, and you try to build a proof of concept as soon as possible - the minimum viable product - and put it out, see what happens, extend it, put it out, see what happens, and so on. You do these quick iterations, and as a result what you end up with is, very often, a monolith architecture, where all the parts and all the components of the system are really strongly interconnected.

> It becomes harder and harder to maintain that system, to then add new features and build it out, because it slows down the development process. That's normal. Happens to many companies

and you really need to start thinking about how you come out of this. Usually what happens is that when you have the market traction, then it's all good. You know that people want the product. You're then trying to, in parallel, build a plan of how to change the architecture so that it would be more scalable for the future growth that you foresee.

There's a lot of desire in the tech team really to spend a little bit more time on things and build things more properly. It's all for a good reason. On the other hand, you have the market pressure. You need to go out quick, quick, quick. So balancing between the two is really hard."

The growing importance of the smart phone as a consumer device was also recognised.

"For some time, we were monitoring the need. We knew it was coming. We knew that there were even some countries, like China for example, where they even skip the whole era of computers and went mobile directly. We were monitoring the demand from our customers, but at some point it got to a place where we just had to invest some of our resources in building a mobile solution."

To keep adoption as simple as possible for consumers, Realeyes waited for the right technological advances.

"We tried to make it as easy and as natural as possible for consumers we are testing for emotional engagement, when they're consuming video content online. For that, we wanted it to be all browser based, and not require people to install any additional software.

Technologically, this was possible on the desktop, laptop environment, but it wasn't for quite some time, on mobile. It was Android platform. That was our first, which enabled us to do that

> with Apple following just last year, which finally allowed us to enable a full measurement of emotional engagement on mobile devices."

Realeyes constantly scans the horizon for new opportunities.

> "We're tracking a number of different commercial measurements on all of the customers that we have. We started to try to identify which industries we have our biggest opportunities in. What is our strategy with the small customers, in terms of the amount of investment, the type of skills that would be required to bring them on board? What kind of investments do we do with the large customers and how do we need to drive product development in our whole company to be able to align it with the expectations of the large customers? We still see equally good opportunities in both and we're trying to pursue both right now."

There is a sharp focus on organisational evolution.

> "So, a couple of important factors to take into account. One is that you have to grow the organisational structure with the company, and so you will constantly need to review that and make sure that you have a structure in place that makes sense and is fit for the product and for the clients that you're having. Sometimes this can be neglected and left to happen naturally."

> "The other thing to pay attention to is if there's a cultural change. So, when you are just a few people and you all know each other, and all friends - you talk the same language, and you understand each other very easily. When you start growing, then the culture is going to change. The way you're working is gradually becoming more professional, and that can have an effect on the people that have been in the company from the start, in the way they work in this environment. The type of people that you bring on board to join in the company when it needs changing, is very important."

Perhaps one of the most significant step changes for Realeyes, as it increased control and IPR, was the transition from the initial outsourced development team to an internal one.

> *"We received our first round of funding and when that happened, we needed to build a proof of concept prototype. To do that, we decided that 'Okay, let's outsource and build that proof of concept, and see if it's going to have a market traction'. We thought that's going to be a short project that does not require us hiring teams and building teams in the company yet. This is why we went down that route, and then as it happened, the proof of concept was successful. We wanted to build it further. There were certain components which we couldn't outsource anymore. We had to build them in-house, so we kept the outsourcing team and started hiring people internally as well. For a while we had both running in parallel. So, it was gradually happening as part of our reaction to the market."*

Increasing demands for communication were also recognised.

> *"In a small company, everybody knows what they're talking about because everybody works very closely. As you grow, this changes, and people talk, as a result, less and less to each other. It's very easy to have silos in the company where there are groups of people that are working on a project, but they're not really aware of what's happening elsewhere in the company, if they're even working on the right thing, and how is that linking with some of the activities that are happening elsewhere. So, it is really, really important to think about the strategy of communication in this growing environment. There's a need to communicate more, and more, and more. Sometimes it feels like you're over communicating, or that this is completely unnecessary, or sometimes even that it's a waste of time. Over and over, I come to the conclusion that there's no such thing as over communication."*

To underpin this theme of communication, Elnar and his co-founders extended the leadership team.

> *"We started to build a leadership layer in the company. First by, bringing some of the key people in the team up to the challenge. Then, also by bringing some people from the outside, focussing on individuals who have been successful in their roles in other large organisations, with the similar spirit, and have gone through a similar growth experience. Not quite the startup that we are, but companies that have been startups before and grew to bigger companies today. So right now, we do have that management layer in place and we do have regular communication structures in place as well to make sure we have a full alignment across the whole management team in the company."*

This provided the founders some precious time to steer the business.

> *"It is so easy to lose the vision of the big things if you're just constantly focussing on the day to day."*

Oyvind Henriksen, Founder and CEO, Poq
Established in 2011, Poq has achieved 1015% growth and in 2017, was awarded a place in the Fast 50. Defining and building App Commerce software, Poq enables leading retailers to forge deeper and more valuable customer relationships, increase insight, engagement, conversion and revenue, whilst decreasing costs, risks and implementation time.

The idea for Poq came from Oyvind Henriksen's 10 years' experience as CTO of a Norwegian e-commerce agency. He came to London, where he met the other founders and noticed that most retailers were making apps in the same way that he used to make websites in the '90s. This was by hand, from the ground up each time. Most websites had since moved on to big platforms, such as Magento or Demandware, but there were no platforms available for apps. Furthermore, the founders realised that app commerce was about engagement, retention and long-term relationships with clients. This was very different to e-commerce or mobile commerce.

Poq was born to provide a commerce platform for native apps harnessing the increasingly popular Software as a Service (SaaS) model.

> *"The benefit you get from Software as a Service is you're really quick to market. You can provision the software. It works out of the box and then it's really fairly easy to integrate with. You get access to great online tools, so there's a complete management system. There's a developer centre. There's all of these things so you can manage your own app, without necessarily having to call anyone. It's being kept always up to date."*

It built an ecosystem of partners, with many plug and play integrations, which lowered the barrier to entry even further and differentiated Poq from the agency approach. Having established an impressive list of independent fashion brands and smaller retail chains, real growth started when Poq won a contract for an Android app from their first enterprise customer, House of Fraser.

> *"The interesting thing there, our breakthrough, was that we were really flexible. Being an early stage start-up, we can iterate really quickly on our proposition. We could learn what enterprise customers really needed from us. We had this really quick interaction of having a meeting with them, trying to discover what they needed to see for the next meeting, developing champions on the client side, trying to work out from them what would be the next step, the hurdles that they would need to get us through, because we realised they really wanted a platform approach. They didn't want another agency, and everyone we were up against were agencies."*

> *"So, we essentially dropped everything, did not do anything else for three, four months or something like that. That was the only thing we did was just deliver for House of Fraser, get their app out in time for Christmas trading. We succeeded really, really well with a lot of effort from everyone. Everyone worked late. We put everyone into all of the demos, a lot of those things. It was really successful. Then, we spent the next half a year doing the iOS version of it as well.*
>
> *We essentially spent a year on just levelling up for House of Fraser, and it was a huge achievement and it opened up a lot of doors for us. But it couldn't have worked if we were not small enough to actually be able to rally everyone around our mission."*

The founders managed the risk and reaped the rewards.

> *"You make choices, you factor in the risk and decide what to do based on that. You can have a good outcome but a bad decision, or you can have a good decision but a bad outcome. You just won't know. So you just do the best you can, and you don't expect to be right all the time. So we try to be deliberate. We try to plan ahead. We try to be very intentional about everything we do. We also try to be enterprising, so we jump on opportunities. We let everything go and we go for it, and it's about managing that."*
>
> *"We've done it many times, I think. It's a habit of really navigating as close as you can on the edge of what is acceptable risk."*

Establishing a strong portfolio of over 20 brands, Poq managed the accompanying challenges of scaling.

> *"It's much easier to deliver software for one client, or for a couple of clients, or even for one leading client, and then a few following clients. Missguided took a very active driving seat in the direction of our company, because they are amazing and really good at what they do, a very successful company.*

> *We had a few companies like that, who were quite innovative. We work with Made.com, the furniture company, and they've done great things. I think it's really interesting, because you can learn from each other. All the companies can learn from each other, but they do pull in slightly different directions. You need to manage that. It just requires a whole lot of homework to get ahead of what clients actually want, and work out a way to productise it.*
>
> *It's inherently very difficult to do work for one client and then replicate it across everyone else, because you tend to, from a product management perspective, you tend to be pulled too far in one direction, and it doesn't fit with the rest of your clients. I think this is one of the things that we've done really well in the last year is to consolidate properly and have a rigorous product management process ... and be able to make that fit really well with lots of customers, and not just one or two."*

Deployment was simplified by the newly available Windows Azure cloud platform.

> *"In my previous company, we were building our own servers. We had our own server room. We were connecting all of the things manually. It was a huge relief just opening up Windows Azure, creating our first servers, and deploying things, and just leveraging everything from a cloud infrastructure point of view. It keeps things super simple. It makes everything so much easier. Because there's preworked things that you can just piece together and make them work, rather than having to recode everything and rebuild everything. So it's a lot simpler than it was before."*

The founding team invested significantly in understanding the culture they wished to create at Poq.

> *"We had the benefit of having four founders in our team, that bring different perspectives and also a bit of long-term thinking by*

retreating a little bit away from the core business, and going out for dinner together, and so forth. That has enabled us to think a bit long-term sometimes. One thing we did pretty early, and this was Michael's idea, was we connected to this guy called Gabbi at Multiple. He identified more the culture of the company and the values and all of these things. I think it was really good to do that exercise of finding the identity of the company. I think that was key, a very important thing that we did that early. It took a lot of time and resources and so forth, but it has paid huge dividends in the longer term."

With this understanding, a Head of People was hired who provided clear guidance on how best to build the team.

"You can take the values of the company, the culture of the company, and you can expose people to it throughout the hiring process to make sure that you get the best fit of people from a very, very early stage. So not in the final interview position, but really early. Make the fit from a cultural perspective, a really essential part of it."

This enabled Poq to find the right talent and develop its unique skill set through continuous team based learning.

"Having that ability to find great talent and find a way to onboard people and develop people into their careers and so forth, has been really important for us in that scaling capacity, because we do have a fantastic team. We have great culture. We have very talented people, with a really unique skill set. Not many people know about apps, and app commerce. In London, outside of these walls, it's still fairly new as a category ... tricky to recruit for, because the talent is scarce. I think having really good quality in the team that then sits together in London, learning together, developing together, has been very important. We do rely on passion and talent as our primary solution for scaling. As an engineer, my default will always

be to go for, 'Let's codify process for everything.' But actually the opposite has been more effective for us. There's still a little bit of process, but we probably have had more success than I thought by just having great talent in the team."

As the organisation evolved, heavy investment in communication across teams helped avoid silos.

"Traditionally, we always had a lunch table, so we always had lunch together as a team. When we were small enough, everyone had lunch at the same time, but that didn't scale. We also do team events. We do Friday all-hands meetings, with drinks. We do Town Hall questions. We do updates from the teams. We do demos of the improvised developments. We do announcements and so forth, and people can hang out in that area for a few hours before they take the weekend off."

Work-life balance is an important value for the company with a strong belief that this is essential for sustained success.

"I'm Norwegian, so I care a lot about work-life balance. We wanted to kind of kick off on Monday saying, 'This is what we want to do in the week.' And then wrap up on Friday, saying, 'Okay, we've done that. Go home.' to give people enough time to rest."

"I appreciate the Silicon Valley culture of just living together, working together as a team of 10 people for eight years and then IPOing, but it's not quite our style. So, for me, it's not a sprint, it's a marathon. So you want to make sure that you can run that, and get paced for a long amount of time."

The reasons for Poq's sustained success to date are clear.

"Having a plan, ... a very super clear vision that this is what we want to do, having thought and having done enough homework on

... that just made our real decision later much, much easier."

"We had some advice really early on to not just focus on product, because being a designer and an engineer by background ... I would just tend to think that if you build a great product, great things will happen. But we realised very early on that you actually need to be quite customer-led, and you can innovate with customers, because customers will tell you, while you work with them, what they need you to do.

So, I think we found that balance, more or less. I think us just being able to channel that customer learning and feed it into product was probably the key thing for us. Inherently a difficult thing to do, which is why I think that it's a valuable company, because we're doing something that is inherently difficult and hard for other people to do."

Joel Davis, CEO & Founder, Mighty Social
With five years' sustained high growth and two consecutive Fast 50 awards (2016/17), Mighty Social along with sister brand agency:2, is Europe's fastest growing social ad tech company. The business serves its innovative AI driven Ad Tech platform, the ATOM. This achieves tremendous reductions in media wastage, whilst delivering impressive ROI to some of the world's most innovative brands, including Barbie, JLL, Fisher-Price, Pan Macmillan, Verisure, Worldpay and Mega Bloks. Mighty Social operates in over 13 countries.

As a marketing director, Joel Davis started to see the impact social media was having compared with display and other opportunities for digital media. This insight and experience led him and Sharon Baker to found agency:2, Europe's first full service social media company.

agency:2's first client was Newham Council's 2012 Olympic Games Unit, who were promoting audio guides for the Olympic Park to residents. Having demonstrated how forums can generate leads and downloads, agency:2 started working with other major customers including Intercontinental Hotels. At a time when Facebook advertising was very much in its infancy, agency:2 was exploring early opportunities in social media marketing.

Seeing the power of social advertising to scale social media, agency:2 provided scalable solutions for big brands.

> *"When Facebook started getting a much more sophisticated ad offering, it really made a big difference to our business and also to the pitching process, because up until then, the big questions were, 'What is social media? What is Web 2.0? How can it help drive return on investment?'. It's about getting the right message in front of the right people, and Facebook's algorithms, and massive reach, and their sophisticated system allowed the starting of a new wave of advertising."*

Growth took off dramatically when the business received funding to build an ad tech platform.

> *"We built the first version of it called the 'Social Insight Engine'. And that was collecting a lot of survey data and social data, combining it together. The survey data was very interesting, because it allowed us to ask people questions like, 'What are you looking to buy next, or do next?' So, for example, we would get the data of people who were looking to move home, or renovate their home, and combine that with social data, which meant that we could then target people who were looking to buy something, but knowing things like their personality traits, their interests, age, gender, location, and starting to do some very clever stuff."*

> *"That opened up a new world for us really, because not only was it*

> *a smarter way of advertising, it also became quite a unique opportunity for us to sell to more companies, because we weren't a 'me too' company anymore. We suddenly had some very unique technology, which was very, very useful to the market. And that was our USP, essentially."*

> *"Once we had the technology, we started winning some big accounts and when we asked the client why they chose us, they said it's the technology, because it was just different to the other businesses."*

This success fuelled rapid growth in the team, seeing it double four years in a row. Throughout, the business maintained its clear entrepreneurial culture.

> *"Culturally, it's been an interesting one, because obviously going literally from four, to eight, to sixteen, and when you get to some big numbers, like when we got to twelve, thirteen people, it was suddenly ... we can't celebrate everybody's birthday, ... we can't go to a restaurant because suddenly you need a big table. And then we got to twenty, twenty-two, and suddenly we needed a different level of management.*

> *So, it's been incredible. I mean, as a co-founder and a director, the challenges of having a very fast, entrepreneurial, agile type culture, where everyone is working together ... trying to find the strengths of everybody to keep them doing different things all the time, whilst the need for more process and due diligence, is a fine balance. It's still incredibly important. We still believe that if we're not agile and entrepreneurial enough, we won't survive. We have to continually push, always push. Take the risk, but do things like we were when we were only four or six people. The same energy."*

Hiring focussed on finding highly capable graduates with the right cultural fit and then shaping roles for them.

> "We generally hire quite young individuals out of university with good degrees, so we know they're intelligent, and have the right mindset. So, the personality and fast learners, and then we bring them into a role. We're very happy for them to move around. When they first join us, they don't necessarily know what they want to do. Do they want more creative, or analytical, or technical, project management? So, we hire on the back of the person first, not the role, and then, if they're the right person, we'll find a role for them."

The organisation has retained a flat structure with support for staff mobility around different functional areas.

> "In our business we have to create good looking ads, and we have to target the right people with those good looking ads. You can't separate those two distinct processes. And then there's ... the selling and the reporting, but it's all so intertwined, that splitting it up, although it's an easy option, is not an option that we've taken. We do encourage people, always, to move around. We don't want silos. Sometimes we do, from a line management point of view, because we have to ... too difficult for one person to manage everybody ... But, we don't want to have too many separate teams."

Joel and Sharon have built their management team from within, looking for sound judgment and good decision-making abilities.

> "I think people need to be pushed, so we give responsibility quite early on. They need a career path, otherwise they'll move on, which is fair enough for some people, but actually if we can help them in their career, then they can help us create and continue the culture that we desire."

> "Your intuition tells you, more than anything else, and you know if it's right or wrong. If you make a decision that doesn't feel right, you know it will come back and bite you ... it's very important that

people have good decision-making powers. Otherwise, you become a liability in a business as managers, because you keep having to check decisions."

For sustained growth, the ability to continue to take calculated risks remains key.

"Although the risks we take are bigger, because our balance sheet is relatively strong, we've got more room to make more risky decisions. Because if it doesn't pay off, it's not going to cause the company to collapse. But, it means that we've always got the confidence of knowing, if it's the wrong decision, that's okay. So, we still try to create an environment of taking some risks ... We have to, because if we don't, then competitors will."

Excluding the modest funding for the ad tech platform, the business has been entirely self-funded and managed cash flow very carefully in order to sustain growth.

"Cash flow is even more important when you're growing fast, because you never have an opportunity to catch up, because the next quarter is bigger than the quarter before. So, it probably took until about a year ago where, from a cash flow point of view, we don't have to look at it every single day. Because, we're growing on average about eighty to ninety percent a year. In particular Q4 is challenging, because there's a lot of spending goes through Q4. By January or February, when most of the money comes in, there is a bit of a relief, I have to say."

In addition to winning the Deloitte UK Technology Fast 50 twice, the business has won many other accolades including the Inc. and Shorty Awards. Not yet a household name, these provide much appreciated recognition for the whole team.

"This year we won the Inc. award. The top 5000 fastest growing

> companies in Europe. We did very, very well. The team should be very, very proud of their work. Last year we won the Shorty Awards for the best use of Facebook. The Shorty Awards is like the Oscars of social media. So in New York, all the biggest and finest companies present their best social media campaign, and we won it for a campaign we did here in the UK for Thomas the Tank Engine. It wasn't about something dubious like awareness, it was something very, very specific, which is driving sales and proving it. We were up against mainly big American companies, the biggest brands you could ever imagine, and we had this little campaign in the UK."

> "We used our technology to target mums with children who are likely to want to go to the cinema. Being very clever, being smart. The experience of a parent, for example, in a newsfeed, is very noisy. The parents are anxious, they're busy, they haven't got much time, they've seen lots and lots of ads continually. So, if you can be very specific with finding the right creative for each of the relevant mums, then you can make a massive difference."

Looking forward, there is further potential for colossal growth.

> "Something like ninety percent of all the increase of ad spending is only going to two players … Google and Facebook. Social media and search, is digital media. That's it. We decided to focus on the social media part of it, which is fine, we need to focus. But, we've picked a good horse."

> "From a brand's point of view, they save a lot of money, because so much money is wasted on media. The click-through rates, on average, are way under 0.1%, which means 99.9% of all media is essentially wasted. And that is so much money! In Facebook advertising alone, you're talking about 60 billion dollars a year. We're using our technology to have a massive reduction on that wastage, because there's a huge opportunity for businesses to do it in a better way."

> **Stephen Upstone, CEO and Founder, LoopMe**
> Before founding LoopMe, Stephen Upstone and Marco Van de Bergh worked together for 11 years on mobile video advertising. After years building successful businesses and learning many lessons along the way, they decided to apply their hard won knowledge to a new venture. Founded in 2012, LoopMe's mission is to close the loop on brand advertising, using data and artificial intelligence. In 2017, it was placed 12th in the Fast 50 with 1,825% growth and is now the largest mobile-first video advertising platform.

Stephen and Marco had observed a move towards consumption of more and more rich and video content on mobile devices. Realising that the smartphone was not only becoming a more important screen, they recognised it was also an important collector of data. They saw the potential to close the loop on brand marketing, and named the business LoopMe.

Their first big challenge was to build data about consumers and start to predict what they would do. Having achieved this they began closing the loop on brand marketing.

This vision has remained fairly consistent since the business began, with Marco and a small team, in a shed in Stephen's back garden in north London. LoopMe's core service grew from the UK into a European business before expanding across the US. Based on their previous experience, the founders hired a relatively big sales team of six in New York, to break through. The business has now grown to over 200 people, operating in 50 different geographies in Asia, across Europe and multiple cities in the US, with most of the revenue coming from the US.

LoopMe focussed on very big brand advertisers at agencies that traditionally had spent money on television advertising. As consumers moved to digital devices, so too did the brand ad budget. Very quickly consumption moved from desktop to mobile.

LoopMe allowed big brands to adapt ideas originally created for television advertising and modify them to work on the small screen. Huge amounts of data about consumers and how they were interacting and reacting to content could now be collected. An AI self-learning system optimised the results. All was handled within GDPR and the compliance expected by any large brand.

LoopMe's Data Management Platform can collect a trillion new data points a day. The entire underlying intelligence system updates continuously, learning over time, growing smarter and smarter and can now place ads in two billion devices around the world.

The current engineering team of 80, includes a large data science team of 25 who share a background similar to Google DeepMind. The UK has proven both a very strong base and global lead for product design, artificial intelligence and data science.

> *"We've been relatively fortunate at being able to hire a lot of the best talent across the industry. And I think there are a couple of reasons for that. We are fast growing, but we're also working in an interesting part of the business. We are innovating with mobile data and mobile products around video and artificial intelligence and some of the hardest people to find are good AI software developers these days. But the thing that we can give them is access to huge data sets and products that are already deployed across 2 billion people.*
>
> *Many other companies might be solving very niche problems, tweaking a financial instrument, not really seen by anyone and the data sets might not be as big or exciting. And so that and the ability to work with the latest types of deep learning, and work with the experienced team here, has meant that even within that, which is probably the toughest part to hire for, we've been successful at securing very strong talent."*

LoopMe's software development team, created in the Ukraine using relationships from previous businesses, has drawn on the talent pool that existed within the Soviet Union.

> *"When we started, we used an outsourcing firm, but it was one that allowed us to actually hire our own team and manage them. So that gave us a kind of fast HR function plus office space etc. in the Ukraine. And then as we have grown out, we have internally an HR function. In fact the last year, we hired 100 people around the globe, including sales, technology, and we didn't use a single external recruiter for that. We had an internal recruitment team based out of London and in the Ukraine as well."*

The remote development team started with little domain knowledge but was soon nurtured by Marco.

> *"Having a co-founder who has been probably the best technologist that I've worked with previously, who again has a very strong product marketing, deep technical experience with a very strong product marketing bent; having worked and developed products actually over the in the Valley and worked with me before, meant that we could create products that they might not have all the market context, but with the right kind of scoping and development cycles. It's worked exceptionally well and we'd certainly support other companies taking the same route and do the same again if we set up another company in the future."*

As experienced founders, Stephen and Marco have delegated effectively to the wider leadership team.

> *"One of the most important things, is to empower people to make decisions and grow and run their own parts of the business, whether it's sales or marketing or product development. Empowered teams work much more strongly."*

To grow the company culture in an organic way, promotion has been strongly biased internally.

> *"We've looked on the whole to try and promote internally where possible. You should have an almost unfair advantage of getting a role if you're already here than compared to not being here. Not that we haven't also brought in a lot of great talent externally.*
>
> *That's led us to our own people. We ask them what they think about the team and the culture. A lot of the things that come back would be about us being smart and innovative and fast-moving, and many of the other things you'd expect. But one that they fed back to us, is that it also felt like a family, a family environment, and that I think is a very strong part of our culture. That makes us stronger. We've been very fortunate to build that culture on a global basis."*

Transparent communication across the team is deeply valued.

> *"We try to be fairly transparent as well. Every time we have a board meeting, we then discuss on a video call around the entire 200 people, the staff, what the board was asking, what was kind of key issues. They won't always be understood or appreciated by everyone. We'll try and give people a forum then to ask questions. We try and promote internally any successes, whether or not they're coming from the client teams or marketing, data science, sales, etc. So we trying to celebrate successes together and yes, that seems to definitely be working well for us."*

As it grew, Stephen's previous experience helped him structure the international team.

> *"We resisted what would have been a normal thing to do ... to hire a big new senior team over in the US, and have the two teams almost go off and do their own thing. We almost built them in an*

integrated way. And that wasn't through the lack of funds, it was trying to keep this clear message and clear way of working across all the different teams. And we even moved people from certain parts of the business. So I had a few people who moved from the UK to the US. I think that's hugely important. We fly a lot between different hubs. People tend to come to the hubs of New York, London and the Ukraine, rather than everyone go to the satellite offices. But occasionally, there'll be some of us from the senior team that will go to the satellite offices as well."

"So far, that seems to be working pretty well, but it's definitely something that requires a lot of attention. And as you go from 200 people to 300, 400 or so, that's something we'll have to keep an eye on."

Based on the many lessons learnt in previous endeavours, the LoopMe founders have successfully steered the business.

"I feel that we made a lot of business mistakes, learning business wisdom, from previous companies. Obviously there are things that will happen during the course of business, where there'll be an error or an outage or a product piece or something, especially in the early days. You'll hire some people who don't work out as well. There aren't many things that I can look at today and say, 'Oh I would never have done that the way that I did it, or the way that we did it'. They are mostly understandable mistakes that you'd have to almost do.

There's a great example that AI kind of learns by making mistakes, and actually it's very similar to babies how they learn how to walk initially. They fall over and they bang their head and they sort of do all these things. That improves and helps you to learn and helps you to get better and better and better, and faster and faster."

The founders' passion and enthusiasm remains undiminished today.

> "I'm always hugely enthusiastic about the experience of just diving in and starting. I started relatively early on in my first start-up, I wasn't a founder, but was kind of employee number one in a couple of different cases. And I think that there's a great kind of comfort that you can get from having started with nothing and ended up with something quite substantial. And that's going from that kind of zero, zero product, an idea that you're going to shape."

> "The first idea doesn't have to be perfect. I think with our kind of core idea and vision of closing the loop on brand advertising and taking feedback, it hasn't changed massively. But there are many, many tweaks we've made to the business or big market shifts that helped propel our business. So I think to some extent, you have to get out there and do it and continue to be agile and continue to ask questions. That same curiosity that drove you to be a founder in the first place, shouldn't just dissipate as time goes on. I'm sure that many of the people from very large and successful businesses continue asking questions. Apple would be a very obvious example. So don't delay in going out and getting started. Continue to keep asking questions."

Stephen's advice is never to underestimate the immense commitment required to achieve this level of success.

> "It is going to be very hard though. What looks like a relatively easy journey from a shed to a large business now today, you have a lot of very tough points within that. You're fighting to bring in funding or you had a disappointing quarter that didn't grow like the last one did or something happened you weren't expecting. There are definitely a lot of those kind of challenges along the way. You just have to keep pushing through. But I don't think there's a better career path or job or something that would be more exciting than starting a business and growing a business. I think that doing that from the United Kingdom today is a very interesting prospect as well."

3. MY STORY

The greatest satisfaction for me has always been to take a new idea and make it happen. Throughout my life, I have measured success in terms of both my achievements and by the positive differences these have made to me and those around me. But perhaps what makes an achievement more valuable are the mistakes and learnings that happened along the way. An inevitable part of the process, these challenges must be endured and overcome with persistence and commitment.

Whilst studying for my science A levels, my neighbour John, a research metallurgist, invited me to visit his laboratory. He shared his passion for materials science, showing me how he tested exotic metals and alloys to destruction as part of a jet turbine development project. I was hooked. This was it - I was going to be a research scientist!

I went on to complete an honours degree, a PhD and four years of post-doctoral research in digital imaging. But after 10 years in academia, I came to a shocking realisation. Like an accelerating bullet, I had been shot out of the educational gun barrel but had completely missed the target. Although the work had been of high value, it was unlikely to bear fruit for decades. I wanted to make a difference 'right here, right now'.

I took the big leap into industry and joined a medical imaging start-up which was developing miniaturised ultrasound devices. Imaging arteries from the inside, these had the potential to dramatically reduce the necessity for open heart surgery. This highly capable, multidisciplinary team was creating an entirely new medical imaging system from the ground up. I joined a team of three developers and built the end to end software. The system performed well in several clinical trials and I felt very privileged to join the founding Cardiologist as he worked on patients in the angioplasty theatre. I was seeing the results of my work in action – where it really mattered.

The bigger picture for the company however, was rather more problematic. The most significant technical challenge was microengineering tiny identical piezo-electric crystals, 64 of which were assembled around a cylindrical centre to produce a circular array 1mm in diameter. Due to patient safety requirements, the resultant imaging device was single-use only. Potentially great for the company revenue, but this required the ability to mass produce these devices. A very experienced team had been assembled to achieve this, some members recruited from leading edge microengineering teams at British Aerospace. After several years of development, sufficient volumes became available for clinical trials.

Unfortunately, the expectations of the investors (a large medical device company and several venture capitalists) were far higher. Requiring a fast production ramp up, an experienced general manager was brought in to scale the business. Recruitment and investment in production machinery accelerated. Ambitious plans were implemented.

All this was achieved without sufficient attention to limitations in the probe design and build processes, which were simply not ready. The financial runway ran out and although further funding was secured, ultimately the root problems remained unaddressed. The imaging device side of the business was reduced back to a minimal research team again. At an all-hands meeting, the Chairman broke the devastating news. We were all to return to our desks where we would find a letter informing us whether or not we still had a job. I shall never forget that day and in the year that followed, I saw many of my valued colleagues lose their jobs. On several occasions I was told I might not be paid at the end of the month. Despite my intense feelings of loyalty to the company, I decided enough was enough and sought another opportunity.

The experience of working in a small tech business and my software development skills opened up an exciting opportunity to join another company of a similar size. However, this one was serving real customers and on the cusp of enormous success. Over several years, Metrica had developed its proprietary relational database capable of storing large multidimensional arrays of data, together with a rich library of mathematical and statistical functions. This was sold as a horizontal solution to analyse large datasets for a wide range of customers including car engine manufacturers, utility companies and NASA. Rapid growth began when the business pivoted to focus on GSM mobile phone network performance reporting, at a time of rapid rollout and intense competition between the main operators. This vertical product became mission critical to the customers and sold for more than ten times the original price.

I worked closely with the brilliant founder and technical director. Still very much hands on, he led our small talented team, steering us whilst contributing significantly to product development. Over the following two years we grew the team carefully, doubling in size. The business was acquired by a large Canadian communications company and we celebrated in style with a Christmas weekend at the Gleneagles Hotel. We moved to bigger offices in the centre of Richmond and the development team was allocated the penthouse floor with a wonderful view. The creative culture had grown within the team. It truly was a fabulous time.

Not long after, the parent company brought in a new energetic and ambitious CEO and experienced professional managers were hired. The business committed to ISO9001 accreditation with the goal of attracting more enterprise customers. The founders started to leave and for me, slowly, almost imperceptibly to start with, the vivid colours turned to shades of grey.

We hired more rapidly, accepting that we would have to lower the bar to build the capacity for larger projects and customers. Our lead web developer was offered a lucrative contract to work at the Financial Times. The company did little to retain him and this key developer was replaced by a team of engineers who could not achieve the same productivity.

Previously relying on peer testing and customer support by the core team, separate speciality test and support teams were created. The new recruits were very collaborative and committed but saw their value as introducing more structure and process learnt in bigger, more traditional companies. Despite being promoted to junior management level, I quickly became frustrated. I found my time shifting significantly from hands-on development to supporting team members, writing design specifications and producing quality procedures. Shortly after the founders left, I accepted an offer to join a consultancy based in the City.

Just before moving on, I set up a small crack team of the best developers to work with an accomplished product manager on a new data aggregation product. We minimised the formal processes and the team flew, reminding me what true creativity and productivity a high performance team could achieve.

I joined TRS Consulting to help one of the founders start an e-commerce practice supported by software product development. In retrospect, timing could not have been much worse. In 1999, most potential customers were obsessed with the impending threat of the 'millennium bug'. The appetite for new products and development was very low and the practice did not win significant business. The two founders parted and the business went into a tail spin. After striving hard for more than a year, I heard about another start-up where one of my former Metrica colleagues worked. This too was on the brink of significant expansion.

I moved to Orbis at the beginning of the new millennium and was immediately impressed by the immense ability, spirit and commitment of the team. There was a real buzz of excitement across the 20 or so people that made up the business. The founders had clearly invested significantly in building this high energy culture.

The company had been bootstrapped by its three founders, initially working from one of their living rooms in west London. They had secured an exclusive distribution deal with a US based application server technology company. This enabled them to provide dynamic data to web sites which had previously not been much more than static digital brochures. Customers included a cable TV company, mobile phone network, leading newspapers and sports bookmakers.

The business retained the IPR for its solutions. It became clear that there was huge growth potential in sports betting with a significant number of bookmakers wanting to extend their businesses on line. The product OpenBet was born with a proven scalable licensing model and significant additional customisation work.

The core technical team centred around a gifted leader whose focus was on the rapid product development and resilience of the solutions. The engineers were extremely bright, dedicated and creative and not afraid to speak their minds even though most were only a few years out of university and with limited experience. Seeing how I supported and guided them, James the founding MD, asked me to manage and build the team.

Determined not to repeat the mistakes experienced in previous start-ups, I continued to hire only the best talent. This maintained very high standards, with an expectation that new starters got up to speed and contributed within a few weeks, exerting minimal load on the existing team. We accepted some projects were under-resourced but avoided the trap of just 'making up the numbers'.

Key to growth was a close partnership with a top recruitment agency, Rocfish, and together we created a strong pipeline of talent. With a stream of gifted engineers joining the business, I set about ensuring the growing team continued to improve their ways of working together. It was essential to maintain momentum and not lose productivity if the business was to continue delivering to its increasing customer base.

Creating new teams around each of the customers, I identified leaders with deep domain knowledge, strong mentoring skills and sound judgement. The teams quickly established high levels of trust with their customers, updating their sites frequently, meeting with them to review the success of new features and to plan more. Although all work was done in our offices, customers told us that it was like having their own in-house team. Indeed, one customer was so impressed with our ability to consistently deliver that it made a serious offer to buy the company.

The founders decided on a different path, which led to a deal with NDS, the television technology business arm of the News Corporation group. NDS saw sports betting as a flagship for their new interactive services where live sports were key to their Pay TV clients. Their CEO, former head of R&D at IBM, understood that we knew our market and how to exploit it. Whilst providing financial support and business leads, he allowed us to continue to be masters of our own destiny.

We moved to a bigger office and continued to hire rapidly whilst maintaining standards using our proven recruitment engine. I built teams to create new products, including a telebetting call centre application and casino games. Within a year, revenues rose from £3.5 million to £11.5 million, taking growth to 999% over just 4 years. For two consecutive years, we were awarded a place in the prestigious Deloitte UK Technology Fast 50.

However, there were still mistakes along the way. With increasing sums of money passing through our customer sites and continuous pressure on the development teams, I created a support team and hired an experienced manager who in cultural terms, looked a good fit. He in turn hired experienced support engineers. Although this team introduced some much needed process including support ticket management, it did not develop sufficient understanding of the solutions and members became go-betweens. This delayed responses to the customer whilst loading the development team further.

I replaced the manager and persuaded experienced developers to join the team. Domain and product knowledge was shared across the new team and members empowered to fix issues directly before handing off product updates to the development team. The service became a 'one stop shop' for support issues and was rated highly both by customers and the business.

This experience reinforced my belief that primarily it is better to grow from within, augment from outside when required, and stay close to the management team. This avoids the 'leave it to the grown ups' syndrome. We continued to maintain the original values of the business and explore how we could improve our ways of working. We avoided transplanting established processes from bigger companies and didn't ask the 'grown ups' to come in and fix things. We grew up ourselves.

The founders completed their earnout and left, having made huge personal sacrifices to grow the company. Shortly after, I joined NDS having been very impressed both by their ethos and approach.

NDS, a multinational company with over 3,000 staff, was on the face of it, very different to the start-ups I had known. However, they shared many of the values and had brought together talented individuals into high performing teams. The business had delivered multiple waves of innovation to the industry. Having secured Pay TV against piracy with leading edge cryptography and smart card solutions, it provided the end to end systems that took satellite TV into the digital age. It had also created the disk based personal video recorder that transformed the way people watched TV. The company was led by a very charismatic and technical CEO who understood the importance of the team. Presence and communication were both very important to him. Whichever world office he visited, he regularly walked the floors speaking to team members to gather their views and see their progress.

On taking charge of the Digital TV Metadata R&D teams in the UK, it became clear to me that TV was evolving rapidly from scheduled shows to on demand. Well before the launch of the iPhone and iPad, I saw that the future for consumers would be to watch what they wanted, when and wherever they wanted. We set about working on this immediately.

The two original R&D centres in Israel and the UK were joined by the US, a rapidly growing centre in India, and then by France and Denmark. The combined strength of the teams drew on global talent pools and became immense. Competition between the teams was encouraged to stimulate creativity and drive momentum forward. As the different teams continued to grow, some of this competition became counterproductive with similar solutions appearing in several locations.

The senior team decided to reboot R&D into two global teams. The smaller one focussed on longer term innovation whilst the other worked mainly on near term incremental research and development. When asked which team I preferred to join, I chose the second, following my personal North Star to make a difference 'right here, right now'.

I joined the leadership of a new global division for the back end TV systems, responsible for the European teams. At our first meeting in Bangalore we shared our visions for the future. To avoid costly duplications of work, I proposed the creation of a small global team of product managers that would steer this vision locally in a shared direction. Successfully implementing this, we created similar global teams to coordinate software architecture and to deliver major programmes of work.

Whilst not perfect, we successfully led the division through the transformation from satellite to hybrid online video. I focussed my teams on the key content services: curation, management, discovery and delivery. My streaming team created an adaptive bit rate video streaming solution that enabled delivery of live video streams across the Internet. I still remember with pride, demonstrating this technology to the Executive in a remote country hotel, streaming live Italian news via ropey Wi-Fi. These solutions are in use today by some of the world's biggest TV operators.

NDS was bought by Permira in 2009 and sold three years later to a global tech giant for $5 billion with an ROI of x2.3. I was now, seemingly, a long way from my start-up roots. But it would be a mistake to characterise it this way. The same principles of bringing together the best talent, with the right working practices and leadership, still applied. The challenges of growth and communication between teams in different rooms are very similar to those faced by those working in different countries. These principles allow a start-up to grow rapidly, sustain success and continue to grow into a multinational.

After 10 years learning how to successfully scale a global business, I left and found myself at a crossroads. Should I seek further employment or start my own business? Having supplied solutions to Sky for 15 years, an unmissable opportunity presented itself to complete and launch its new online video platform. After much deliberation, I accepted, taking development and operational responsibilities and inheriting a leading edge agile engineering team working at scale. In just over a year, we doubled the team whilst further raising its engineering standards and operational awareness. This was critical to the success of a platform that was required to deliver 24x7 under any expected load. As the team grew, I developed emerging leaders and ensured they proved themselves in the right roles.

Within two years, we launched the new in-house platform, extending it for international deployment on private and public clouds. We supported the migration of all Sky's online propositions and stabilised the remnants of the original platform. All this was achieved under increasing record levels of load without any significant core platform outages.

Whilst 100% committed to these revolutionary changes, I still sought my own professional transformation. Having delivered all that I had committed to, I decided to move on, return to my roots and help grow small innovative businesses for sustained success.

I have worked with many founders and shared both their failures and triumphs. I have seen the sacrifices they have made, the joy and pride of great achievements and the despair as their legacy slipped away and fell apart. I set up Digital Hunters to walk alongside more founders, to help them navigate through the minefield of growth and discover their own paths to success.

DAVID WICKS

PART II: THE FOUNDERS' WORLD

1. A DIFFERENT VIEW

The Founder, Entrepreneur, Hunter

If you ask a group of people "What is an entrepreneur?", you are likely to get many different answers. They might refer to famous, successful visionaries such as Steve Jobs, Elon Musk or Mark Zuckerberg. Maybe they will point you to the Pied Piper founders featured on the hit show *Silicon Valley* or the many, varied participants who pitch their businesses on BBC's *Dragons' Den*.

The classic image may be of a brilliant, usually young, perhaps geeky, graduate of a top university. After a few years' experience at a big consultancy, they have a great vision, sell it to eager investors and build their empire. Certainly, there are founders who fit this bill. There are others who, for many years, worked in a particular industry. They identified a gap, saw an opportunity and using their own financial resources, successfully took it.

Whatever the entrepreneur's background, many never succeed in building a flourishing business. One common misconception is that luck makes the difference between triumph and failure. In my experience, this could not be further from the truth. This misunderstanding arises from the belief that being in the right place at the right time happens just by chance. The reality is that the entrepreneur chooses the place, judges the right time, identifies the opportunities and delivers. These individuals see the world in a very different way to most, envisaging futures previously unimagined, recognising potential in new technologies that few others appreciate. It's nothing to do with luck. Entrepreneurs are 'hunters' in the business world.

It takes significant skill to spot the right opportunity and even more to deliver profitably. Successful hunters often have many scars from previous mistakes and these guide their way forward. Some become serial entrepreneurs, learning from their failures and achievements, moving on when they wish to seek a new challenge. Others are inspired by those for whom they have worked, love the culture and life and want to do this for themselves. Some businesses actively encourage staff to do this, perhaps even providing financial support. A number of entrepreneurs may be motivated only by the wealth that success can bring. Many are driven by the desire to make their mark on the world, to build something that no one else has, to leave a legacy.

Most founders start a business in a small team of at least two, covering business strategy, sales and technology between them. Some start-up factories assist individual founders to find others with complementary skills who can complete the team. Other founders, with the ability to sell and deliver, start out and succeed alone, finding it easier to be answerable only to themselves. Whatever the makeup of the team, it must be strong, resilient and adaptable if it is to ride the waves and survive inevitable storms.

Once the business takes off, many realise they do not have all the skills required for grow. At this early stage, selection of the right people to augment the team is absolutely vital. Professionals with start-up experience can be a major asset, if they are willing to adapt to the specific needs of the business. However, experts often believe they add the most value by providing existing models of working that have been proven elsewhere. If done prescriptively, as a grown up might show a young child, they are likely to cause serious problems. Equally, it is dangerous for founders to adopt the mantle of the stubborn teenager who ignores all advice, believing they know everything. Growing up within the business (with guidance) is usually the best approach.

Another common misconception is that entrepreneurs are big risk takers. Certainly, they embrace risk in the desire to make a difference and change the status quo. But the most successful are the more calculated risk takers, taking increasingly bigger risks as their business grows, yielding larger rewards. This is backed by confidence in their own resilience if things go wrong.

Hunting for new opportunities inevitably involves risk. Risk taking is about moving out of comfort zones, away from what is known and predictable. When building a new enterprise, it is essential to effect change. But risk is clearly not limited only to start-ups. Many large incumbents have seen their market domination taken away by disruptors after failing to adapt. Avoiding change carries its own significant risks.

Exploring the domain

Usually, successful founders start with a vision of what they want to build or change within a specific domain, then make a plan to achieve this. Some have significant experience and a super clear vision of opportunities, their potential value and how to realise them. Others understand the potential for a particular solution or technology but do not know which application will be the most valuable. Regardless of the level of clarity in the original vision, if they are to gain maximum value there will invariably be an ongoing process of exploration. To find where the most value lies, this is likely to involve the creation of new solutions followed by quick tests and iterations. As Napoleon instructed his generals before battle, 'Engage and See'. In his book 'The Lean Startup'[1], Eric Ries documents this now classic process for discovering high value opportunities.

Sometimes, one particular application of a solution fixes a critical problem within a domain. Its value is orders of magnitude greater than any other. If this opportunity is taken quickly and effectively, it can lead to the creation and domination of a new market and phenomenal growth. This move from 'horizontal' to 'vertical' solution can transform a business, particularly if it has created and protected its own intellectual property. As a business grows and builds its customer base, entire product families and ecosystems can be built, further protecting it against commoditisation. Spotting these opportunities requires a good understanding of customers' real needs and desires.

One of the most difficult experiences for the hunter is the realisation that a golden opportunity has been missed. However, chasing too many opportunities at once, without sufficient focus, is a recipe for failure. The ability to see an opportunity, evaluate it according to the business vision and plan, then choose whether or not to take it, is another essential skill. In retrospect, a founder may discover that they did not choose the most valuable direction and this is the benefit of hindsight. We have to make decisions and live with them, otherwise, we become forever paralysed by the fear of 'getting it wrong'.

The Power of the Small

In May 1940, World War II raged. On the beaches of Dunkirk, over 338,00 British and Allied soldiers were trapped, encircled by German troops. In response to this, as part of 'Operation Dynamo', the British Government sent out an unprecedented call to any civilian who owned a boat capable of operating in shallow waters. Owners of such vessels soon discovered that their mission was to ferry these cornered troops from the beach to larger naval ships who, unable to come any closer, waited in deeper waters.

Very quickly, an 850-strong flotilla, known as 'the little ships' was mustered. A jumbled assortment of vessels including car ferries, pleasure craft, lifeboats and paddle steamers all set sail for France, many with civilians at the helm. Tiny fishing boats, such as the 'Tamzine', only 14 feet long, also took part in this heroic venture.

Together, over a period of nine gruelling days, many thousands of helpless troops were rescued. Out of this miraculous real life story has emerged the everyday phrase 'Dunkirk Spirit' which epitomises courage, determination and solidarity shown in the face of difficult or dangerous situations.

Today, small businesses who have a clear focus on emerging opportunities can exploit these far more adeptly that larger companies. Like those 'little ships', they can take advantage of their compact size, act quickly, change direction rapidly and venture into waters not open to larger, more established businesses.

Like the momentous Dunkirk rescue fleet, small businesses can join forces to achieve a shared goal far faster than larger ones can. Collaboration between start-ups is common for mutual benefit, particularly when these companies share the same space, investor or incubator. For example, several years before merging, Paddle worked closely with Andy Savage's Calq and shared complementary solutions.

Sometimes, an entrepreneur who sees significant and valuable gaps in the solutions provided by incumbents, actively seeks to fill these. This disruptive approach can be particularly effective when the incumbents are too big to spend time on these initially small opportunities. Like colossal ocean going tankers, large companies are unable to stop and turn into small ports. Their shareholders' mission is to drive them towards only the biggest 'ports of opportunity'.

Notable exceptions exist where market leaders have spawned smaller businesses to move quickly in an emerging market; Sky's creation of NowTV being an excellent example. However, many large businesses choose to acquire their potential disruptors once they have proven themselves, providing lucrative exit opportunities for founders.

2. FAILURES

"Failure should be our teacher, not our undertaker"

Denis Waitley, the Psychology of Success.[2]

The inspiring stories from founders of the Deloitte UK Technology Fast 50 demonstrate many of the paths to success and sustained growth. There are a multitude of traps that businesses can fall into as they traverse the growth minefield. Unfortunately, many fail to avoid them and are never seen again.

Failure is an unfortunate constant in the start-up story, and the data is damning. According to British Insurer RSA[3], more than half of small UK businesses don't survive beyond five years. The Office for National Statistics and CEBR report[4] that only 3.8% of small companies grow to become medium-sized ones[a].

This is only part of the overall economic picture. In March 2018, restructuring consultancy Begbies Traynor reported that almost half a million UK businesses were experiencing 'significant' financial distress, up 33% over the 12 months since Article 50 was triggered to leave the EU[5].

How can this grim situation be mitigated? According to the Harvard Business School[6], whilst only 18% of first time entrepreneurs succeed, this rises to 20% when entrepreneurs have previously failed and leaps to 30% when they have previously succeeded. Clearly, experience counts. But why do start-ups fail? Beyond the obvious triggers for bankruptcy such as insufficient cash flow – what are the root causes?

---

[a] Using the OECD definition: small = 10 to 49 employees, medium = 50-249.

There is a wide range of root causes, but some stand out:

- **Scaling too soon** — Relatively easy to manage in small scale start-ups, once growth happens, governance and fiscal discipline becomes a multi-headed monster.

- **Focus** — As the number of customers increases rapidly, it is very easy to lose focus and chase too many ideas or requests.

- **Talent** — When hiring, the imperative to grow drives compromise and recruitment of the wrong talent, diluting the team's quality.

- **Perfection** — Spending too long perfecting the product before testing it with real customers.

- **Failure to adapt** — Inability to pivot direction towards solutions that have real customer value.

- **No IPR** — Failing to protect intellectual property early enough.

- **Too much control** — With insufficient delegation, growing demands on the business become overwhelming.

- **Losing customers** — Chasing new customers without paying sufficient attention to retain existing ones.

- **Culture** — Dissonance between the founders' culture and ethics and those of stakeholders.

For businesses that had followed the 'Get Big Fast' model[7], the Dotcom crash in the early noughties proved a very painful lesson. Indeed, the Start-up Genome Project[8] found that 74% of high growth internet start-ups fail due to premature scaling. This study also concluded that start-ups that scale at the right time, grow around 20 times faster than those that scale prematurely.

At my first start-up in medical imaging, I learnt this the hard way when the business attempted to mass produce the ultrasound devices before a build process was ready. There have also been a number of well documented higher profile failures. Webvan[9], valued at $1.2 billion in 1999, expanded geographically before proving its business model. Two years later, it shut down losing over $800 million investment.

Throughout my career I have seen many fatal mistakes:

- Insufficient attention to design and build processes, causing financial meltdown
- Hiring conservative managers who favour order and documented process over productivity
- Subpar hiring, resulting in a poor choice of new talent, which dilutes performant teams
- Breakdown of founders' working relationships, causing loss of direction and business collapse
- Burnt out founders who regret a premature exit and subsequent lost legacy
- Cultural dissonance and destruction of company ethics and values

However, failure was indeed my teacher and not my undertaker. I used earlier learnings to help Orbis grow by 999% over four years and make the Deloitte UK Technology Fast 50 for two consecutive years. I led and scaled R&D teams at a high growth multinational tech business, later purchased by a global US tech leader for $5 billion.

What follows is *The Map of Growth* - a distillation of my experience and that of fellow winners of the Deloitte UK Technology Fast 50. It shows founders how to discover their own path to sustained success.

3. THE MAP OF GROWTH

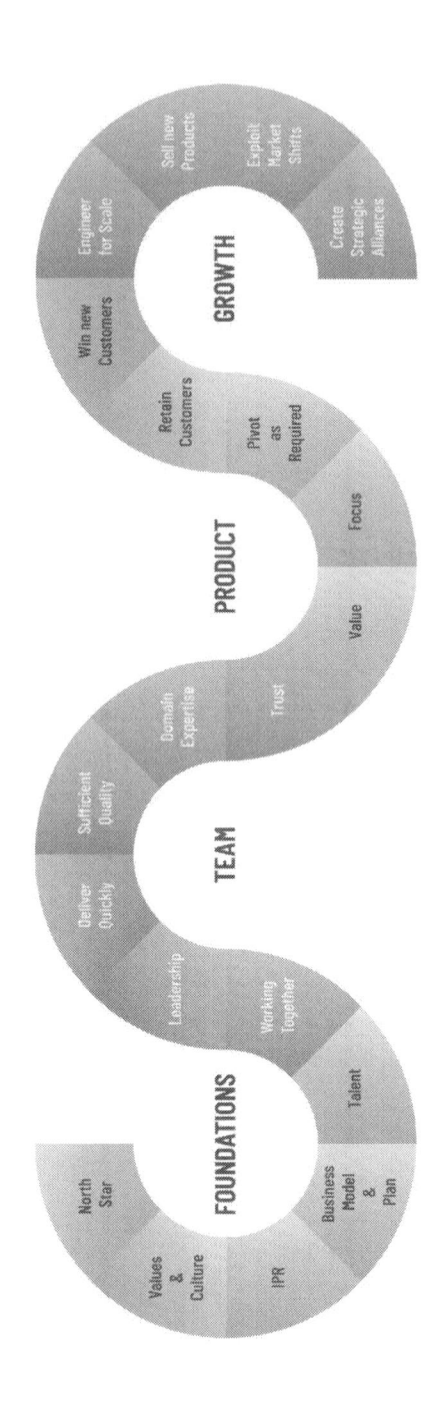

GROWTH: Sell new Products, Exploit Market Shifts, Engineer for Scale, Create Strategic Alliances, Win new Customers

PRODUCT: Retain Customers, Pivot as Required, Focus, Value, Trust, Domain Expertise

TEAM: Sufficient Quality, Deliver Quickly, Leadership, Working Together

FOUNDATIONS: North Star, Values & Culture, IPR, Business Model & Plan, Talent

The first part of this book celebrated the success of some of the highest growth tech businesses in the UK over the past 20 years. Not only have these businesses found the right paths that sustain growth, they have avoided many of the traps that can lead to failure. Now, we will plot out these paths using *The Map of Growth*. This shows the key steps to take from initial vision (or North Star) all the way to sustained growth.

Encompassing four stages, the journey begins with the essential **Foundations**, followed by **Team**, **Product** and finally **Growth**. No matter which step a business takes, it must be mindful of all previous steps that led to it. In many cases, significant issues can be traced back to a problem that occurred at an earlier step, pointing to a need to revisit that step. For example, a product focus issue often relates to a lack of shared vision and leadership across the business.

As well as looking back, it is as important to anticipate the steps ahead and to prepare for them. A business might still be hunting for its high value product with constrained focussed tests. But to avoid significant re-investment, it must be mindful of the future requirement to scale bestselling solutions.

Like a jet pilot, a successful founder must complete pre-flight checks before setting off and accelerating down the runway. Otherwise, when inevitable turbulence hits during 'flight', cracks can appear and disaster may ensue!

FOUNDATIONS

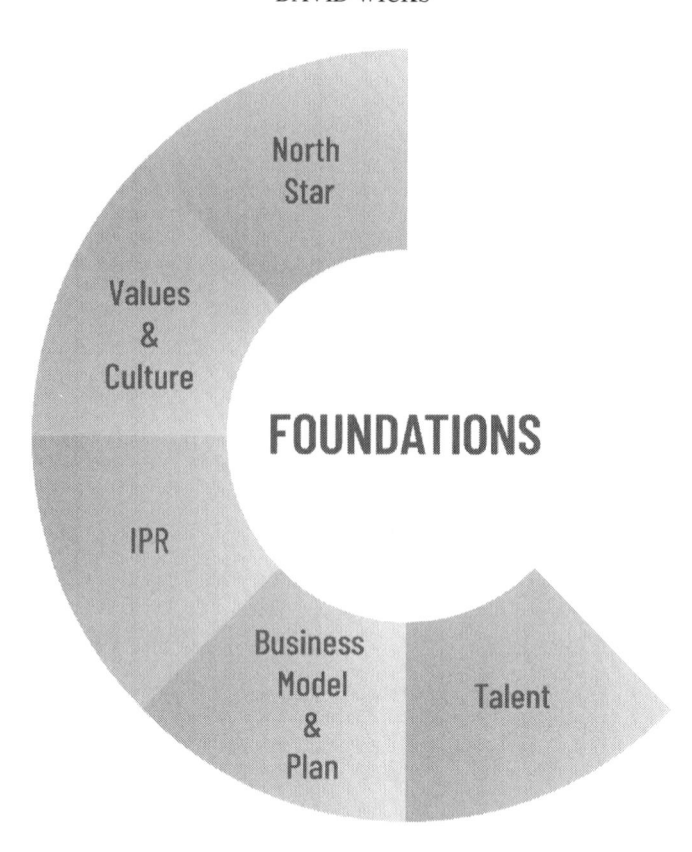

- North Star
- Values & Culture
- IPR
- Business Model & Plan
- Talent

Strong foundations are essential to sustained business success and growth. Based on my own experience and that of other successful tech founders, there are a number of key foundation stones that must be in place if the business is to sustain high growth and not collapse under its own demands. These form the first stage of *The Map of Growth* and will evolve to support the changing needs of the business as it scales within the stages that follow.

Without these foundations, founders are likely to be overwhelmed by rapidly increasing calls on their time. They see their business fracture and spiral downward. Their dreams remain just dreams or worse still, turn into nightmares.

North Star (There to Guide)

In May 1961, President John F. Kennedy made a speech to the US Congress stating:

> *"I believe that this nation should commit itself to achieving the goal, before this decade is out, of landing a man on the moon and returning him safely to the Earth."*

During a visit to the NASA space centre the following year, the President famously noticed a caretaker carrying a broom. He stopped and introducing himself to the man, asked him what his job was. The caretaker thought for a moment and proudly replied:

> *"Well, Mr. President ... I'm helping put a man on the moon."*

Regardless of what job you do, you are contributing to a greater vision evolving within your business and your life. When everyone in a team adopts this approach and sense of purpose, amazing things can be achieved.

Once stated and understood, the vision or North Star enables the whole organisation to focus on a common direction. In the early stages, this provides the focus and direction for optimal speed needed to bring a solution to market rapidly. When customer numbers accelerate, it allows the whole business to maintain focus and not be dispersed across a wide range of customer demands, which can lead to paralysis.

Close, strong customer relationships are crucially important and can generate many promising ideas. However, no matter how big or productive the business, with limited resources a choice must be made about which ideas to take forward. Ideas that move away from the vision can be quickly discounted with minimal debate.

As the team grows significantly and specialises, perhaps in different locations, that vision provides a rallying call to unify all. It also ensures that those not in customer facing roles, still understand what contribution they make and why their high performance matters.

Receipt Bank steers its continuous innovation, and evaluates each idea by asking the question "Does this save the customer time?". Skyscanner have grown their service and acquired multiple businesses by following their North Star to 'Put the traveller first'.

Not all founders start with a clear vision for their business. Some begin as if on a quest, with a belief that there is great opportunity if they explore a particular path. Nervecentre took this approach with the application of mobile technologies to acute health care.

Nevertheless, there is huge value in asking "What is our North Star or Vision?" . Even if the answer is "We don't have one (yet)", the business will move forward with this awareness.

VALUES AND CULTURE

Founders build a business based on their personal values. From these emerges a unique company culture that shapes the individual roles, teams and core working practices that will become critical to growth.

Organisational culture is instigated by the founders, shaped by the leadership and based on the core values of the whole team. It determines how a business grows and continues to succeed. High performance depends on cultural coherence across the business.

At a very early stage, Poq's founders consciously evaluated their culture. They believe that this has helped guide every business decision, particularly when taking significant risks.

Four core culture types have been identified by William Schneider[10]:

- *Control* - values certainty, order, stability, discipline and accumulation. It is resistant to change but will mandate it when necessary. Individuals usually stay within a function (e.g. engineering, consulting, operations) with specialities channelled into the service of functions. Power is based on hierarchical position.

- *Collaboration* - values synergy, diversity, pragmatism and spontaneity. It is open to change that comes from the team. Individuals serve in numerous functions. Power is based on relationships.

- *Competence* - values professionalism, expertise, continuous improvement and individual freedom. It is open to change driven by achievement goals. Individuals stay within a technical speciality with functions channelled into the service of specialities. Power is based on expertise.

- *Cultivation* - values growth and development, commitment, involvement, creativity and the freedom to make mistakes. Change is embraced and automatic. Individuals can serve numerous functions or foci, within a specific function or technical speciality. Power is based on charisma.

High growth cultures must embrace change. In my experience, most tech start-ups are either *cultivation* or *collaboration* cultures. As they grow, elements of the *competence* culture may well emerge. The *control* culture is more prevalent in larger, usually multinational, businesses. However, they may be more commonplace in countries that already exhibit this culture and those that emerge from other *control* cultures such as the military. Multinational businesses must embrace the different cultures from their distributed teams, benefiting from their relative strengths, whilst sharing common values across the organisation.

Hiring people with shared values and culture is key to a growing business. Indeed, culture can become a significant selling point in a competitive market, particularly for ethical based businesses. An individual who needs a *control* culture in order to perform, will seriously struggle in *collaboration* and *cultivation* cultures and may create local dissonances, significantly impacting on their team's performance. A person with the values of a *cultivation* culture will hate being part of an organisation that most values control and is very unlikely to perform to their full potential.

Ways of working in teams are intrinsically linked to their culture. Much favoured agile development methodologies have many variants determined by the culture of the organisations that adopt them. This is most challenging in *control* cultures. In worst cases, agile language may be used alongside behaviour totally contrary to the fundamental principles, leading to widespread confusion.

Both individual and organisational development are driven by culture. Receipt Bank highly values personal responsibility which drives its whole approach to learning, development and advancement. Everyone is responsible for their own performance reviews.

Major business issues, sometimes terminal, can arise when a business with a particular culture acquires another with a very different one. Cultural synergies and a common North Star led to Skyscanner's successful acquisition of six smaller businesses.

Culture is not a badge or an 'inspirational' poster hung on an office wall. It is what happens in practice. Some successful founders document their values and cultures to reinforce them. Others rely on providing personal examples and word of mouth. Whatever the case, if a business is to sustain success, its real values and culture must be known and understood across the whole team.

EventVue built online communities to improve conference networking by enabling attendees to search for and connect with others. Despite £455k funding, the company closed in 2010 after less than three years. Significant cultural mistakes were cited[11], including not 'failing fast' and early hiring compromises that chose expediency over talent and competency.

CDBaby is an online record store and independent music distributor. Its founder, Derek Silvers, has shared his story of attempted mutiny within his team[12]. He discovered that the team had shifted its focus from serving clients to its own entitlements and benefits. Derek acknowledged becoming too distant from his management team and not nipping problems in the bud early enough.

At Metrica, I saw for myself how culture can shift when founders leave. For me, the colour faded to grey and productivity plateaued. Focus shifted from individual creativity, contribution and close teamwork to following traditional 'best practices' and the creation of organisational silos.

IPR

Most founders of successful high growth businesses own the Intellectual Property Rights (IPR) for their solutions. Without IPR, a business is vulnerable to competition. A key asset for businesses, it is particularly important when creating a new market and establishing a leading market share. When a business finds its unique selling proposition, it should always seek to protect it.

A business may own IPR from the start. Universities that create IPR through research, increasingly look to realise the commercial potential through spin-off companies. My first start-up, Intravascular Research, is one example. Although ultimately the business was unsuccessful, the IPR has subsequently been sold a number of times.

When a business retains IPR for a solution delivered to a customer, it can productise and sell that same solution to multiple customers. The perpetual right to use the solution can be paid for as a licence and is the basis for a scalable business model. Orbis successfully achieved this with OpenBet.

In the personal finance management space, Wesabe was the first in a new wave of companies to provide these services. It established a strong market lead only to lose this to Mint when it launched 10 months later[13]. Had Wesabe developed a unique selling proposition protected by IPR, there might well have been a very different outcome.

Business Model

Rapid growth depends on a strong scalable business model. Detailed guides on how to create and develop a business model are available elsewhere[14]. Here is a very high level overview which provides key pointers to a high growth model.

In 2004, an MIT Sloan School of Management study identified four basic business model types[15]:

- **Creator**
  The creator usually takes existing technology stacks and libraries and transforms these into a saleable finished product. This can be licensed and installed on customer devices and platforms. Pricing is usually scaled according to the number of users and devices or a measure of the underlying services such as server CPUs. Many software product companies have followed this model.

- **Distributor**
  A distributor buys a product and resells it to others, often providing value-added services. Orbis Technology started with this model, using Bluestone's Sapphire Web, before becoming a creator with OpenBet.

- **Landlord**
  A landlord represents any company that sells the temporary use of its assets. In recent years, the Software as a Service (SaaS) model has increased in popularity, reducing time to market and up front capital costs. This allows businesses to pay a subscription based on the usage of the services and is supported by a growing number of public cloud services. Both Paddle and Realeyes adopted Amazon Web Services (AWS) whereas Poq harnessed Microsoft Azure,

benefiting many enterprise retail customers who required app commerce.

- **Broker**
  Brokers perform a service by matching buyers with sellers of goods and services. Whilst distributors buy the products and resell to others, brokers do not take ownership of the assets. Online marketplaces, auctions and best buy search are examples. Skyscanner adopted this model.

Whichever model is used, it can be defined, evaluated and refined simply by using the lean canvas[16]:

Lean Canvas		BUSINESS NAME		25-Jun-2018 Iteration #x
Problem Top 3 problems Describe the top 1-3 problems for the customer segment you work with.	**Solution** Top 3 features Sketch out the top features or capabilities of the solution to each problem.	**Unique Value Proposition** Single, clear, compelling message stating why the business is different and worth paying attention to. This focusses on the key benefits for the product from the customer point of view	**Unfair Advantage** Cannot be easily copied or bought.	**Customer Segments** Target customers
	Key Metrics Key activities you measure		**Channels** Path to customers Inbound and Outbound Direct and Indirect	
Cost Structure Customer Acquisition costs Distribution costs Hosting People, etc			**Revenue Streams** Revenue Model Life Time Value Revenue Gross Margin	
PRODUCT			MARKET	

Unique Value Proposition and Unfair Advantage, at the centre of the canvas, are key to a high growth business. Revenue Streams and Cost Structure will depend on the type of model adopted. All models are optimised and tracked against the chosen growth metrics. These metrics evolve with the business, usually focussing on revenue growth and increased market share followed by profit growth. Externally financed businesses can delay the focus on profit. Self-financed, bootstrapped businesses usually have to track profit from the start. Regular reviews help steer the business towards growth.

BUSINESS PLAN

A plan to execute the business model sets core goals and metric targets, usually incorporating a period for exploration followed by growth. The initial plan can be as straightforward as Paul Volkaert's £5,000 budget for the first 12 months product exploration. It may be determined by the requirements of external investors or one recommended by an incubator or accelerator. There are many excellent books on Lean business planning [17], [18].

Aside from a financial plan, the key elements for successful execution are clear business deliverables, timelines and a resource plan. Successful implementation depends heavily on the accuracy of the estimation of effort required to deliver. In any new venture this can be wildly inaccurate resulting in significant and existential risks to the business. The agile approach to create and maintain a prioritised backlog for deliverables with fast time-boxed incremental delivery, helps minimise these risks. The overall risk is spread across multiple steps during which estimation accuracy increases and incremental risk decreases.

TALENT

At a Startup Grind Europe event in the City of London late 2017, I asked Alice Bentinck, Co-Founder of Entrepreneur First, what the company did to help start-ups recruit. She responded:

> "I wouldn't underestimate the time that goes in to us recruiting those people. We have a talent team working full-time."

"If you have a role to fill, the people you want are probably already in an existing role."

"Ultimately it's around understanding that your job as a founder, your number one job pretty much, is just to hire well. If you hire well, kinda everything just sorts itself out. If you hire badly, you're kinda screwed. So you know that as a founder the majority of your time probably will be spent on sourcing people, screening people, onboarding people. Know that this is a big part of your job. It's probably one of the hardest things our founders face."

At the heart of any great tech business are proactive, talented people with strong analytic and learning skills who thrive in the established culture. As the business grows, more of this talent has to be found in order to build the team. For sustained success all must contribute fully.

Before looking outside the business it is important to understand the strengths, weaknesses and potential of existing people, in particular for leadership roles. Those with the aptitude and interest to lead others should be given the opportunity to prove themselves. Key to success are their mentoring skills and sound judgement. LoopMe ensure that their existing staff have an 'unfair advantage' when filling new roles and opportunities. Mighty Social, similarly, promote from within to develop and retain their talent. Many others have adopted similar approaches.

Having utilised the full potential of an existing team, additional external talent must be found if the organisation is to grow. Some businesses call on already known talent pools. Both LoopMe and Receipt bank took full advantage of this and Nervecenter recruited mainly from its existing network. Other businesses choose to outsource work. In the early stage of prototyping, Realeyes did this but moved the work in-house in order to grow and retain its IPR. Some businesses, including Skyscanner, have acquired others for their teams and expertise as much as for their solutions.

In order to grow rapidly at Metrica, we made the classic mistake of lowering the bar. New engineers were competent and motivated but required far more support from the core team, which resulted in an overall slowdown. Also, not enough was done to retain existing high performers. The net result was a larger team but significantly lower productivity. This is a lesson I have never forgotten.

Eventually, most businesses have to seek new, unknown talent from the job market. Cultural match, fit to an existing team and the clear value they add, are key criteria. Competition for top talent is fierce and many successful growing businesses report this as their number one challenge. To make things worse, the traditional recruitment ecosystem is fundamentally broken.

The past 15 years have seen the rise of massive job sites advertising 10,000s of jobs to which millions of CVs are submitted. The CVs are reduced to keywords and matched against checklists from the job specifications. These sites are used to seek the latest 'hot' skills and ignore all others. Not only that, new technologies and their associated opportunities, are evolving quickly and continuously. What was new and hot just a few months ago will soon be old and cold. Recruitment search filters change continuously.

Worse than this, many businesses just don't know how to attract the talent. They sell themselves to the job market in many ways: cool products, cool offices, cool employees, great social life and awesome promotion opportunities. Although these are important, a rich seam of talent is lost by focussing on the *what* and not the *who* or *why*. Without a holistic view, judgement will always be flawed.

Winners of the Deloitte UK Technology Fast 50 recognise that success depends on the ability to find the right talent at the leading edges of technology. Due to the novelty of those technologies, much of the skills required simply do not exist. They sought a different kind of talent and found it.

The award winners understood that engineers with deep knowledge in one set of technologies, with strong analytic and rapid learning skills can keep up with the rapid tech revolution. But it's not just about technical skills. Fast growing tech companies need highly driven, proactive engineers who get up in the morning determined to make a difference, who would hate to be a small cog in a large machine. They have a strong sense of personal responsibility and desire to achieve. This type of person cannot be found by the outdated CV and Job Spec. checklist approach.

Business and candidate stories provide a much more holistic means for engagement and matching. They focus on the values, aspirations, depth of experience, pride in achievements and love for the domain. Skyscanner, winners of the Fast 50 for seven consecutive years, has a button on its website labelled 'Read our Story'. Those who do will watch the accompanying video and understand who Skyscanner are and why they exist, as well as what they do.

But stories can be much more than just business history. Microsoft have a dedicated web site for company stories in which they tell how they are changing the world. These stories include the work of their Digital Crimes Unit, which partners law enforcement agencies with the aim of defeating cybercrime worldwide. Elon Musk is revolutionising the car industry with the Tesla electric car range. But he still spends significant time sharing his vision for the future, including that of SpaceX, which may one day enable people to live on other planets.

Leading businesses are sharing stories about their past, present and future. Whilst it is imperative that more follow in their footsteps, this is only half the picture. Growing businesses should seek out stories from their candidates. Traditionally, these accounts might be shared at interview but by this time, many potential recruits have already been filtered out - lost to the organisation forever.

Over the past 23 years, I have hired many engineers based on their stories and one in particular stands out. Ted had a CV that would not normally have got through the company filters. He started his career with a string of temporary jobs including martial arts instructor and bouncer at an inner city nightclub. He came to me on the recommendation of one of my team and when I met him, I heard his story. In his broad Cork accent, Ted told me that whilst supporting his wife and three small children, he had returned to college as a mature student. I saw the passion, commitment, maturity and intellect that he would bring to the business. As I write today, Ted, the former nightclub bouncer, is still with that leading software business, still making a key contribution.

Storytelling has the power to transform lives and dramatically increase engagement between businesses and the people who join them, taking career satisfaction to a completely different level. If we embrace the art of storytelling, we will find true talent, wherever it is.

There are many talent pools around the world. All have a limited capacity and wherever tech hubs emerge, competition for top talent becomes fierce. Due to longstanding relationships from previous businesses, both Receipt Bank and LoopMe were able to grow offshore development teams with much lower overheads. Each had founders who provided the necessary support to the remote team.

Rockshore was determined to remain in the UK. Having set up in the north of England, it had to contend with relatively small localised talent pools and huge competition, with 80% churn in staff. Key to their success was the ability to keep the core team together and maintain momentum whilst it renewed the wider team.

Staff retention is critical to sustained growth in an enormously competitive market. Challenging meaningful work with brilliant colleagues, development opportunities, recognition and a fun work environment all help to retain hard earned talent. Enhancing social lives with company entertainments can also be beneficial. The advantage of a smaller company is that staff can make a far more significant contribution to the overall business with a much stronger connection to the larger vision.

Deeply motivated engineers often work long hours to meet an important deadline. But it is important to recognise that this cannot be sustained over prolonged periods, otherwise, exhausted staff stop contributing and eventually leave. Ensuring that people have a work-life balance helps keep burnout at bay. Team creativity and productivity can be maintained by allowing time for experimentation and play. This is the fuel for continuous performance improvement.

[Diagram: An arch shape labeled TEAM in the centre, with segments labelled Deliver Quickly, Sufficient Quality, Leadership, Domain Expertise, Working Together, Trust]

The team is at the heart of sustained success and growth of any business and forms the second stage of *The Map of Growth*. With the right foundations and approach, a high performing team produces the right products at the right time. As discussed earlier, this requires finding and developing the best talent, which is then brought together to create a high performance business.

An organisation goes through several iterations as it grows from the founders and core team, through to multiple teams that may spread over several locations. At each stage, several factors are critical, requiring an approach tailored to that particular phase of development.

WORKING TOGETHER

Putting the right people in the right roles and establishing repeatable, iterative working practices are critical to high performing teams. Often, this happens naturally during the early stages but requires careful attention as growth accelerates.

Culture evolves naturally. In particular, software development culture has been observed to follow a typical progression[19]. I have encountered teams in each of these states:

- **Oblivious** : Work is done in the quickest, most natural way by each individual (whether or not this is the most efficient approach overall). This team might say:

    "We don't think we're performing a process."
    "We don't trust anyone but ourselves."

- **Variable** : The ideal here is the super-programmer who often leads a super-team. This team might say:

    "We do whatever we feel is right."
    "We don't trust managers."

- **Routine** : The prevailing myth here is the super-leader. Success or failure is entirely dependent on the management of the team, which might say:

    "We follow our routines (except when we panic)."
    "We don't trust programmers."

- **Steering** : The team is mainly self-organised and practises continuous learning and improvement. It might say:

    "We choose our routines by the results they produce."

A fundamental mistake is to dismiss most of what has worked before as just chaos, thinking the slate has to be wiped clean. This approach usually looks to hire experienced professionals, the 'grown ups', who bring ready-made proven processes, transplanting them into the team. This can break a highly productive culture.

Awareness of cultural foundations is paramount. Incremental improvements focussed on the highest priority issues, usually team driven, are the best solution. This is built into most agile development methodologies but has to be practised if it is to have the desired results.

As a team grows, specialises and inhabits different spaces, silos can appear, apparently from nowhere. Missed or confused communication across silos can have a enormous impact on both productivity and morale.

The global music streaming service, Spotify, has scaled its teams to maintain speed of delivery, whilst preserving their culture and values of individual accountability and collective responsibility. The organisation is based on *squads*, autonomous full-stack teams of 6-12 engineers with no manager. Loosely coupled with other *squads*, they align together in *tribes,* focussed on delivery and quality of a product. Leadership defines the problems to be solved and why. *Squads* collaborate with each other to find the best solution. Engineers with specific competencies such as web development or performance testing are also members of associated *chapters*. In addition, they can create and join communities of interest called *guilds,* which share knowledge on specific areas.

Whilst it is not recommended to copy this model exactly, the process Spotify followed in order to scale its teams is very enlightening[20]. At Sky, my online video team adopted many of Spotify's principles combined with Scrum and eXtreme Programming. Each high performing team has to find an organisational structure that helps it scale and should appreciate that this will iterate numerous times.

In order to continue growing when local talent is in short supply, it may be necessary to set up additional offices in locations where more talent is available. This might involve subcontracting to other businesses or even acquisitions. Multisite leadership becomes critical. I have seen the disruption that unhealthy competition between distributed teams can cause and I have witnessed the solution when a new global leadership team works as one with shared global goals.

The experienced founders of LoopMe, Receipt Bank and Skyscanner ensured they built a cohesive global leadership team. Without previous experience, Hiroki Takeuchi is creating a distributed team with as much care as he built his first core team.

Leadership & Communication

For a founding team, an early key decision is who the CEO will be. This can be a tough discussion but without it, decision-making is slower. Perhaps the most important leadership role in a tech business, beyond CEO, is that of CTO. This may sound obvious but many businesses have learnt the hard way. A gifted technical CTO with strong people leadership and sales skills is a huge asset to any tech business. This individual becomes the grain of sand around which a business grows its pearl – a world class technical team.

The founding CEOs of both Orbis and LoopMe were clear about the pivotal role their CTOs played in the success of their businesses. Rockshore's founding CEO, on the other hand, described a much harder road when the company had to part ways with its CTO.

The next significant step for founders, requiring outstanding judgment and trust, is to extend the leadership team. Without it, the founding team becomes overwhelmed by the ever increasing demands on their time. They are forced to fire fight constantly, leaving no time to steer the business. High growth will not happen without strong leadership focus. Worse still, growth slows, often leading to a decline and eventually, to business failure.

Growing the leadership team, requires founders to take the same care as if it were their first hire. If a new leader does not share the same values and culture, there will be significant problems. If members of the leadership team do not have open working relationships in which they can challenge each other, they will not perform to the highest level.

Style of leadership depends primarily on the values and culture of founders. Whether the preference is to mandate or to inspire, a high performing business needs clear focus and vision. This must be continuously and clearly communicated by leadership.

As the team grows and is distributed across a larger space, conscious communication becomes more and more important. When the team is small and collocated, this usually happens naturally and by face to face interaction. As the team grows, more structure, preparation and feedback mechanisms are required. It is imperative that new team members understand the business vision, values and behaviours. If the team expands across multiple locations, the leadership must have representatives at each location whilst still acting globally with a shared agenda. This can be achieved by offering regional leadership opportunities to members of the core team with a so called 'DNA transfer'.

As an organisation specialises into different functions, the leadership must span across all teams maintaining the vision and goals of the whole. Leadership can make or break damaging organisational silos.

I have experienced inspirational leaders who command the attention and full commitment of teams across the world with their clear, evolving vision. I have also seen organisations with an executive management layer and precious little leadership or vision. The resultant vacuum creates multiple conflicting fiefdoms where the dominant focus is internal advancement rather than continued success of the overall business. This is followed by phenomenal and oblivious wastage of opportunities and talent. This is not a path I recommend.

Whilst leadership may be challenging during periods of sustained success and growth, it is orders of magnitude more difficult when things go wrong. This may be when a major customer disappears, a big deal is lost to a competitor or a large project fails. Significant investment and work is discarded and the team may have to be shrunk with the loss of valued colleagues. These are the times where clear and honest leadership is essential if the business is to ride the storm. It is critical to manage the sense of doom that can engulf the whole organisation and amplify problems. The role of leadership is to provide perspective and share the longer term view. Jon Slinn demonstrated this clearly at Rockshore. When the tech unicorn, VE Interactive collapsed in 2017, new leadership focussed not on external PR, but on the fundamental organisational values as well as retaining both their team and customers[21].

DELIVER QUICKLY

In the digital age, the needs of customers and markets shift continuously with new solutions that create novel ways of working. Once they have selected their territory, digital hunters must explore the terrain rapidly and find critical customer problems for which they have highly prized solutions.

Gone are the days when most tech businesses could spend months, sometimes years, perfecting a design, building it and launching to widespread acclaim. Only in certain industries such as pharmaceuticals and defence where life is at risk and safety and security are paramount are the old methods appropriate. For everyone else, a process of rapid deployment, testing and refinement is the essential evolutionary approach.

Many 'Agile' development methodologies have emerged to achieve this, most notably Scrum, eXtreme Programming and Lean development. Jim Highsmith summarised these beautifully in 'Agile Software Development Ecosystems'[22]. Scrum provides a framework for a team to deliver at regular intervals, often every 2 weeks. Lean development optimises delivery flow using Kanban and can potentially deliver at any time work is deemed complete.

All follow *The Manifesto for Agile Development*[23] which values:

- **Individuals and interactions** *over* processes and tools
- **Working software** *over* comprehensive documentation
- **Customer collaboration** *over* contract negotiation
- **Responding to change** *over* following a plan.

Although these value statements are over 17 years old, I keep coming back to them as a fundamental guide. Many businesses have adopted the jargon of agile without any real understanding of these values. Even in the past year, I witnessed a FTSE 100 business invest tens of millions of pounds in a large waterfall project, using agile language but adopting the opposite approach for all four values. Consequently, the company has experienced huge delays and is yet to deliver.

Good Enough Quality

Whilst most engineers naturally want to develop a well designed, future-proofed solution, over-engineering an unproven product can be very costly to the small business that can ill afford it. A successful business usually starts by finding basic solutions for quick customer feedback on initial ideas. More rigorous engineering follows for those that gain traction in the market.

Both Paddle and Realeyes described how this process led to success. Their product exploration stage resulted in an inflexible monolithic first solution. But having proven the demand and value, they had the resources to progressively re-engineer the solutions for scale and resilience. I led a similar transition at Sky, replacing its original outsourced online video platform with an in-house solution engineered for scale.

Massive reinvestment in re-engineering can now be avoided by employing web based RESTful architectures and microservices from the start. It is possible to build tightly focussed experimental solutions quickly and evolve these into an extensible, scalable, resilient product or service. Many open source technologies are available to accelerate this. Netflix used this approach to establish global dominance of the entertainment video space and created their own open source libraries for others to adopt.

Many businesses have spent too long developing new ideas, missed their opportunities and failed. This is exemplified by Steve Poland's account of his bootstrapped start-up, MyFavorites[24]. He describes the significant effort that was applied to improve user experience for his app. But with no real users, his team started to lose interest and the business ran out of funding.

A strong engineering team embraces the challenges of delivering solutions sufficient for quick evaluation and understands when to introduce more rigour.

Deep Domain Expertise

To produce the right solutions, a team has to understand customers' real requirements and how technology can be utilised to meet them. Deep knowledge, passion for the domain and an appreciation of the most important problems are all essential.

Nervecentre's first employee was a nurse who now leads a team that has significant clinical experience and steers product development. This team provides invaluable insights based on its fundamental understanding of the National Health Service's operational requirements.

Orbis developed a deep understanding of sports betting, in particular for market making and risk management. This was critical to product development and supported solutions such as betting for ongoing live sports events.

The challenges of transferring domain knowledge to an offshore team are well known. Until this knowledge is accumulated by a remote team, it will be very dependent on existing experts within the business. Understanding of requirements has to be constantly verified and the capacity for creative solutions is significantly impeded.

However, the problem is far wider than this. Founders who choose a domain about which they are ultimately not passionate, will find it extremely challenging to invest time in understanding it. A Y Combinator backed start-up, NewsLabs, and their product NewsTilt provide a clear example[25]. NewsLabs aimed to supply services to help journalists become entrepreneurs and generate revenue online. After 8 months, it closed down with its founders admitting they were just not motivated by news or journalism. Their lack of passion for the domain undermined trust and relationships with potential journalist customers.

TRUST

Large established companies have a known brand and longevity, both of which engender trust. Start-ups do not possess either. Customer trust is earned and based on relationships with the people in the business.

Following years of relationship building and successful deliveries, Nervecentre was pleased to learn this from direct customer feedback. After a long sales cycle and successful delivery to their first enterprise client, Poq established credibility with other large customers. As I write today, there is news of bankruptcy for Cambridge Analytica, which has lost most of its customers following widely publicised accusations of misuse of Facebook data.

Establishing customer trust is essential to long-term customer relationships and growth. It can make or break a business. Customer retention depends on trust that the team understands them and will deliver what they need, when they need it and will not abuse their position.

Trust is also the foundation for a high performing team. In his ground breaking book 'The Five Dysfunctions of a Team'[26], Patrick Lencioni demonstrates how trust between team members allows them to challenge each other openly and develop real commitment and accountability. This leads to a powerful focus on real results. Nervecentre is one clear example of a business that has successfully built its leadership team based on these principles.

GOOD TEAM – GOOD PRODUCT

With the above attributes in place it is possible to create a world class team that has the ability to produce the right products at the right time. The next section looks at the critical elements required for successful product exploration and subsequent growth.

PRODUCT

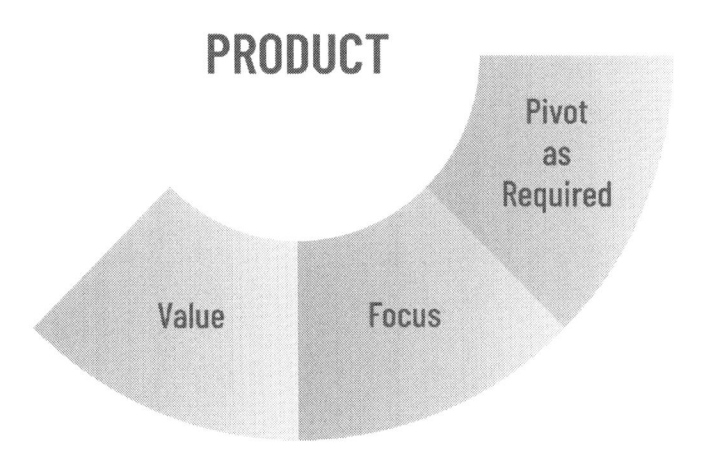

- Value
- Focus
- Pivot as Required

A business will not achieve sustained success and high growth without first identifying and delivering the right products for its chosen market. This forms the third stage of *The Map of Growth*.

Sometimes a solution is clear from the start as it was for Poq when they created app commerce. Within a few weeks of exploration, Receipt Bank learnt that bookkeeping productivity had far more potential than receipt management. For others it can take years, as I saw at both Metrica and Orbis who found a vertical market for their technologies and went on to grow exponentially.

Many successful businesses recognise new waves of technology that could lead them to high growth. When Facebook opened up and developed its digital marketing tools, agency:2 were there to take full advantage. When the smartphone emerged, Rockshore, Nervecentre, LoopMe, Realeyes and Poq all set about tapping its full potential in their chosen domains.

However long it takes and whatever technologies are harnessed, a number of key factors exist that make this hunt for value successful.

Value

High value products solve critical issues for a significant number of customers. From the provider point of view, they are hard to compete with too. This may be due to ownership of key IPR or because the problems are inherently difficult to solve.

Nervecentre's success stems from their ability to determine the real requirements of their customers and then deliver the right solutions, all within the notoriously challenging healthcare sector. Rockshore were able to pull real-time data from ageing legacy systems when all predecessors had failed.

NDS created smart card technology to protect Pay TV content against widespread piracy, assisted by world leading experts, including the RSA algorithm co-inventor, Adi Shamir.

When a general purpose or horizontal product is customised to create a vertical product specific to a particular market and goes on to solve critical issues for that market, its price can increase tenfold. When this also creates a new class of solution or service, the initial market share is very high. Both factors can lead to phenomenal growth as long as delivery can meet increasing demand. I saw this first hand both at Metrica, with the creation of its GSM network reporting solution and at Orbis, with OpenBet.

Often, in mature markets, the incumbent suppliers continue to deliver new features beyond the needs of customers, increasing product complexity and decreasing usability. This leaves the door open for disruptors to enter and focus on simpler immerging needs, thus creating a new market. Clayton Christensen describes this in detail in his book 'The Innovator's Dilemma'[27]. Currently, Paddle are disrupting the software sales market. The long established Pay TV market, where incumbents provide hundreds of channels of scheduled content, is being disrupted globally by Netflix and Amazon Prime.

The product stage in *The Map of Growth* describes the hunt for this value and how to deliver it.

Focus

Perhaps unsurprisingly, one piece of advice that many successful founders offer, is to maintain focus. This enables your solutions to be the best they can in the time available and provides the highest chance of success. Optimal delivery velocity is achieved with a clear focus on what is most likely to generate value. Bootstrapped businesses, in particular, must have this discipline if they are to survive, let alone succeed. Both Receipt Bank and Orbis emphasised the importance of focus to their development.

As the number of customers increases rapidly, it is very easy to lose that focus and chase too many ideas or requests which dilutes the effort and value delivered to customers. Too many parallel activities make it even more difficult to spot the real opportunities and increase dependency on blind luck. Definitely not a recipe for success.

It is easy to be side tracked as you explore particular opportunities, especially when a number of customers are providing feedback, suggestions and requests. Which suggestions are the ones to follow up on? How do you decide?

A North Star, such as 'Put the Traveller First' or 'Save the Customer Time', provides a direction with which to analyse each step for all concerned. Is this step taking us towards (or away) from our North Star? Only those that take you towards should seriously be considered (and then analysed further with respect to relative cost and benefit).

The sooner you realise an idea will not work, the sooner you should discard it. Once it has been delivered to customers it becomes increasingly difficult and expensive to do this. Early feedback can prevent costly mistakes. Nervecentre apply this important principle as part of their working practices.

Saying 'No' to engaged customers is one of the most difficult things to do. Yet, if your customer base is expanding rapidly, you have to accept that 'you can't please all of the people, all of the time'. Attempts to do so will eventually break the business. Realeyes successfully turned away former customers after pivoting from gaze tracking to emotional response measurement.

In order to make a business step change, some companies have taken focus to the extreme. After a few years serving smaller companies, Poq, put everything aside to focus on a single opportunity with their first enterprise customer, House of Fraser. With this successful delivery, Poq built its credibility and engaged other larger customers. Business growth accelerated. The founders understood the risks but were confident they could deliver. They grabbed the opportunity with both hands.

Many start-ups become overwhelmed by the effort and time required to secure additional funding. Whilst that funding may be essential to continuation of the business, so is the success of its products. If finance rounds become all consuming, there is a risk that the business will enter a vicious cycle, seeking external funding when customer generated revenues are insufficient. Andy Savage at Paddle, prioritises building products over securing additional finance, having learnt the hard way.

Pivot as Required

Often, the original vision does not lead to growth. However, exploration of the idea leads to another with far more value and potential. This may be discovery of a solution to a critical customer problem. It may be to exploit a significant market shift or due to the emergence of a new enabling technology.

A successful business consciously pivots towards newly discovered directions. Knowing when to do this can be guided by key practices and associated metrics as described in 'The Lean Startup'[1]. Ongoing discussions and product evaluations with real customers reveal the most critical problems as well as high value solutions.

Deep knowledge of a domain allows founders to see fundamental shifts in the market and accompanying opportunities. Both Realeyes and LoopMe followed the shift of video advertising from traditional TV to Digital/Online.

Facial feature analysis tools led Realeyes to develop an emotional tracking solution that had far more potential than their original gaze tracking product. It also removed the requirement for specialised hardware, opening up larger opportunities.

Blackberry created phones with an integrated miniature keyboard and display, and initially dominated the business market for mobile email. The launch of the iPhone fundamentally changed this market but Blackberry failed to pivot in response. The founder and board member, Mike Lazaridis, resisted a plan to pivot to instant messaging software. He opposed the launch of the Blackberry 10, still stubbornly attached to the physical keyboard as a differentiator. Between 2012 and 2016, a reported[28] $75 billion was lost from the company's valuation.

Once high demand and value has been established, the key is to scale and deliver the solution rapidly before customers look elsewhere or competitors step in and take advantage of the opportunity. Until this happens, the real skill is to walk the fine line between exploration and growth and to identify the transition point.

GROWTH

- Win new Customers
- Engineer for Scale
- Retain Customers
- Sell new Products
- Exploit Market Shifts
- Create Strategic Alliances

Sustained growth is the fourth and final stage on The *Map* of Growth, and follows a six step strategy:

1. **Retain Customers.** Support current customers and help them grow their business.
2. **Win new customers.** Build market share for existing products.
3. **Engineer for Scale.** Ensure solutions continue to deliver to the required service levels under increasing load.
4. **Sell new products**. Develop and deliver new applications and services to customers.
5. **Exploit Market Shifts**. Anticipate and observe market shifts and deliver solutions that meet new needs.
6. **Create strategic alliances.** Partner with or acquire complementary businesses to gain market share and expand reach.

This is a powerful template for any company that seeks high sustained growth. It is one used by NDS for many years, as it built its $5 billion business.

Customer retention and repeat business are key to sustained growth. It is almost impossible to grow substantially through new customers alone. Whilst selling existing solutions to new customers, the business must continue to support and retain existing ones. As customer businesses grow and the number of customers increase, it becomes essential to engineer for scale if levels of service are to be maintained and improved.

When the market matures, competition grows and it becomes increasingly difficult to win new customers. Growth is then driven by developing and selling new products to existing customers, reinforcing retention. This includes identifying and exploiting underlying market shifts.

Market share can also be grown through alliances, acquisitions and global expansion. Over the past 20 years, this has been clearly demonstrated by Skyscanner and other winners of the Deloitte award.

Retain Customers

Customer retention is critical to sustained growth. Loss of any customer moves the business in the opposite direction. Continually replacing lost customers with new ones will expend significant time and resources just to stand still. The cost to retain existing customers is significantly lower than that involved to acquire new ones. Furthermore, providing support services to existing customers can provide a very high margin and if the business model scales with the customer business, growth can be achieved with relatively little additional effort. Businesses with a subscription model continuously monitor customer churn. Businesses that sell to other businesses usually establish account teams dedicated to managing those relationships.

Retention relies upon strong, long-term customer relationships based on trust. Although Skyscanner is not legally liable for the travel sold through its sites, it takes customer support very seriously. It works closely with its suppliers to ensure a great service. Always putting the traveller first has led them to serve over 60M customers each month. Jon Sinn of Rockshore shared how the company lost a small number of customers following extremely difficult deliveries. With a commitment to always deliver (even at a loss), Rockshore successfully retained most of its customer base, including all its original customers.

Win New Customers (and Keep Them)

Given that a business has found a high value product and is in the growth stage, selling to and winning new customers is not usually the biggest challenge. Continuing to satisfy their specific requirements can be far more difficult. Without a strategy and plan to manage this, a business could eventually find itself trapped as it tries to support twenty customers whilst satisfying none. This can easily lead to a death spiral.

When selling to a handful of customers, it is relatively straightforward to deliver to their varying needs and to keep them happy. However, maintaining a different version of a solution for each customer becomes prohibitively expensive as market share grows. Gerald Weinberg[19] plotted a graph of the difficulty in satisfying customers against the number of customers, generating a hump back curve, which peaked at around nine customers. Beyond this number, it becomes almost impossible to satisfy all specific requirements for each customer and a level of standardisation has to be introduced.

Standardisation can take the form of a mass market product such as a desktop office productivity suite. Over time this provides many features to meet the wide range of customer requirements. Unless sufficient attention is paid to usability, this can create incredibly complex solutions that become increasingly difficult to use. It is vulnerable also to disruption by simpler, more targeted, solutions.

For customers at different levels of sophistication and purchasing power, a product family with incremental functionality can help mitigate these risks. The freemium model, in particular, is a powerful approach that wins customers using a free core product and chargeable high value add-ons.

Scaling a product for business customers can be achieved with a common product core that is easily configured and extended. The same product is delivered to all customers with different modules enabled. Further adaptation by the customer, partners or by service teams provide the flexibility that more sophisticated customers demand. I have seen the power of this approach in Metrica, Orbis and NDS.

At some point the business has to consider the size of customer it targets. A relatively small number of large customers can generate impressive revenues but also demands long sales cycles, significant customer relationship management and services. Selling to smaller customers is usually quicker and less demanding but generates lower revenue . This necessitates volume sales and associated marketing. The rise of social media tools has revolutionised this. At the 2017 London Business Show, Tutor2U, an online educational publisher, reported that following the adoption of Facebook marketing tools, it had generated more revenue in the last year than the previous sixteen years combined.

Several businesses that have won the Deloitte award focussed on larger enterprise customers. These include Mighty Social, Poq, LoopMe and Orbis. Others, such as Skyscanner, Receipt Bank, Paddle and GoCardless have scaled with large numbers of small business customers and consumers. Realeyes works with both large and small customers.

Growth can be accelerated by minimising the time and cost for new customers to adopt a product. The Landlord business model with Software as a Service (SaaS) removes the need for significant up-front investment in resources and time with a ready-made infrastructure that scales with the client businesses.

International growth can be a significant business accelerator that extends market reach. In the digital age it is increasingly easy to distribute products across the world. However, knowledge of the different international markets and their cultures is another dimension of deep domain knowledge. Local teams with regional knowledge are essential. LoopMe, Receipt Bank and GoCardless are demonstrating how to achieve this. Their key advice is to fully commit to each new market by building experienced local teams, ensuring they are linked closely to the global leadership. After expanding globally, the acquisition of Skyscanner by the Chinese travel company, Ctrip, has taken this to the next level. Each business must find its own solution for global expansion and evolve the right organisation to support it.

Engineer for Scale

As individual customers grow and the numbers of customers accelerate, it becomes critical to ensure that solutions scale. Successful products must continue to perform as required under increasing load and be resilient to system failures. To achieve this, the solution must be engineered for scalability and resilience to provide its services whenever and wherever they are needed, no matter how many customers are consuming them. Also, it must be extensible to support continued feature enhancement and evolve efficiently without slowing down.

Key architectural approaches and engineering practices are required to achieve this in a cost-efficient manner. Today, most scalable systems harness cloud technologies, which provide many options from public to private cloud. Hybrid variants allow 'cloud bursting' for systems in private infrastructures to scale elastically into public ones under load. Solutions are usually stateless with multiple instances for any given service. Capacity is scaled to support increasing load by adding more instances. If the load varies at different times, it is also possible to remove instances when they are not required, thus managing the cost.

The more parts there are in a system, the greater the number of potential points of failure. Scalable systems should start with the understanding that any individual component can (and probably will) fail at any time and network connectivity can be lost. The overall system must be designed to accommodate these inevitable failures and continue to provide the essential services[29].

From an engineering stand point there are always trade-offs to achieve this. These will be guided by the company's North Star. For a financial institution, security will always be a top priority in order to protect its customers' assets. For an entertainment business, uninterrupted customer consumption is paramount and it will protect the key customer journeys if parts of the system start to fail. This is achieved using technologies such as circuit breakers, redirecting customers to fall back solutions when required. The resiliency of cloud infrastructures also helps protect against major system failures, enabling complete system 'copies' in different locations.

Paddle, Poq and Realeyes benefited enormously as early adopters of cloud technologies. My team at Sky deployed systems across public and private clouds and designed solutions from the ground up for both increased scalability and resilience. This allowed millions of viewers to enjoy uninterrupted live football wherever they were.

SELL NEW PRODUCTS

When a market matures, new customers become increasing harder to win. The path to growth extends to selling new products to existing customers.

A world class development team with a deep understanding of its domain and customers, will naturally continue to identify and create new products. Usually, these are complementary and together can form complete ecosystems, which in turn reinforce customer retention, protecting against commoditisation. NDS understood this when it built a digital TV ecosystem around its leading content security solutions. This also enabled significant pricing flexibility for individual solutions under competitive pressure. Large revenues from key market leading solutions, which are protected by IPR, allow businesses to sell accompanying solutions at a price hard to compete with.

A clear product strategy and continued focus are critical for the business to grow with its customers. Nervecentre has achieved this with its product family for collaboration through mobile solutions. This approach also recognises that customer understanding and acceptance for new solutions is much stronger for products that are related.

Exploit Market Shifts

Even when a business has moved from the exploratory phase to growth, it is still important to remain vigilant to underlying market shifts and to be prepared to capitalise on them. Kodak failed, but not because of any disruptive digital camera technology[30]. They invested in the technology, created a digital camera and understood that photos would be shared online. However, what they did not see was that the new business was online photo sharing, not just a way to grow the existing printing business.

Both Realeyes and LoopMe have capitalised on the market shift of video content from TV to online. NDS also foresaw this and invested heavily in DRM solutions, protecting online content, together with Internet streaming for content delivery.

To maintain a market lead, it can be hugely advantageous to initiate market shifts. Having created the bookkeeping productivity market, Receipt Bank now drive the market shift to real-time accounting and business decision-making.

Create Strategic Alliances

Partnerships with other complementary businesses increase market share and extend reach. Integrations with established partners makes it easier for their customers to adopt your particular solution. GoCardless really took off when it integrated with Kashflow and was used by many of its customers. Poq has many partners to augment its current app commerce solution.

Business acquisition is perhaps the ultimate form of strategic alliance. Skyscanner purchased six smaller companies to extend its service offering significantly and was in turn acquired by Ctrip, which took it to the next level. However, many other acquisitions fail and do not lead to further growth. Cultural dissonances usually have a major influence on the outcome. Skyscanner's successful acquisitions were made possible by the business alignment to a shared North Star. Perhaps the most spectacular failure was the acquisition of 'old media' firm Time Warner by America Online (AOL) in 2000 for $164 billion. Within 18 months the combined value of the company plummeted dramatically from $226 billion to $20 billion[31].

USING THE MAP OF GROWTH

The *Map of Growth* illuminates the key steps from the original business vision to sustained growth. The next section will show how this can be used by any business to navigate its own route to success.

PART III: FINDING YOUR WAY

1. KEY QUESTIONS TO HELP YOU STEER

If you are to sustain high growth, it is important to continually check your readiness for it. You may already be aware of problems that require further investigation and troubleshooting. This chapter provides important questions for you to ask yourself and your team. Reflecting on your responses to these questions, you can establish what has to change to keep you on course for success.

Each founder and business starts from a different place and has their own unique approach. Only you can find real solutions to your specific challenges and problems. What follows is a framework to help you achieve this, along with suggestions to guide your approach.

I have identified 4 key stages as shown in *The Map of Growth*:

- Foundations
- Team
- Product
- Growth

Each stage is presented as a mind map covering a total of 22 topics. For each topic, a number of thought provoking questions will assist you and your team explore what really matters to your business. This will help you focus on what requires attention if you are to achieve lasting high growth.

Although there will be an element of reflection, this is not intended to be an exercise in overthinking. Each key area can be explored through a structured workshop with your leadership, management and functional teams. The output will be a prioritised list of actions preparing you for growth. It is important that each workshop involves everyone likely to take ownership of the resulting actions. If you think an experienced external facilitator will help, then engage one.

For each question listed in the relevant mind map, follow these simple steps:

- **Agree your answer in a time-boxed discussion** - if no answer can be found then assign an action to address this and move on to the next question.

- **Evaluate your answer according to the potential consequences if you take no action** - if these consequences are minor, stop here and move on to the next question.

- **If action is required, decide what is most appropriate** - if the situation is urgent, you may seek a quick fix followed by a more fundamental one when practical.

- **Assign a priority to the action** - the MoSCoW rule is useful here:
    - **M**ust do
    - **S**hould do
    - **C**ould do
    - **W**ould like to do.

    Actions with the bottom two priorities can be ignored.

When you have finished evaluating your key questions and actions, create a prioritised backlog with the most important and urgent at the top.

How you plan to execute these actions, is entirely up to you. If your team practises Scrum or Lean then you may wish to adopt these approaches to deliver them. For example, a business with lean practices could set the maximum number of actions to process at any one time and then manage the backlog using Kanban.

FOUNDATIONS REVIEW

I recommend that both the founders and leadership team participate in the business foundations review as part of the ongoing existing business review cadence. This may range from quarterly to annually. The *Foundations* mind map provides the questions for 6 key areas. You may wish to augment these with questions of your own.

TEAM REVIEW

Team reviews should include both managers and teams responsible for each topic area. These are likely to be engineering, product development and potentially, sales teams. The frequency would ideally fit with existing team improvement reviews. The *Team* mind map provides questions for each of the 6 key topics.

PRODUCT REVIEW

Product reviews are best handled by the leads responsible for prioritising the work of the engineering teams and be part of any ongoing product steering reviews. The *Product* mind map provides questions for each of the 4 key topics.

GROWTH REVIEW

The questions for the growth stage require significant attention from those who have business and technical design leadership responsibilities. Your consideration of these should not wait until the product scope has been defined. The *Growth* mind map includes questions for each of the 6 key topics.

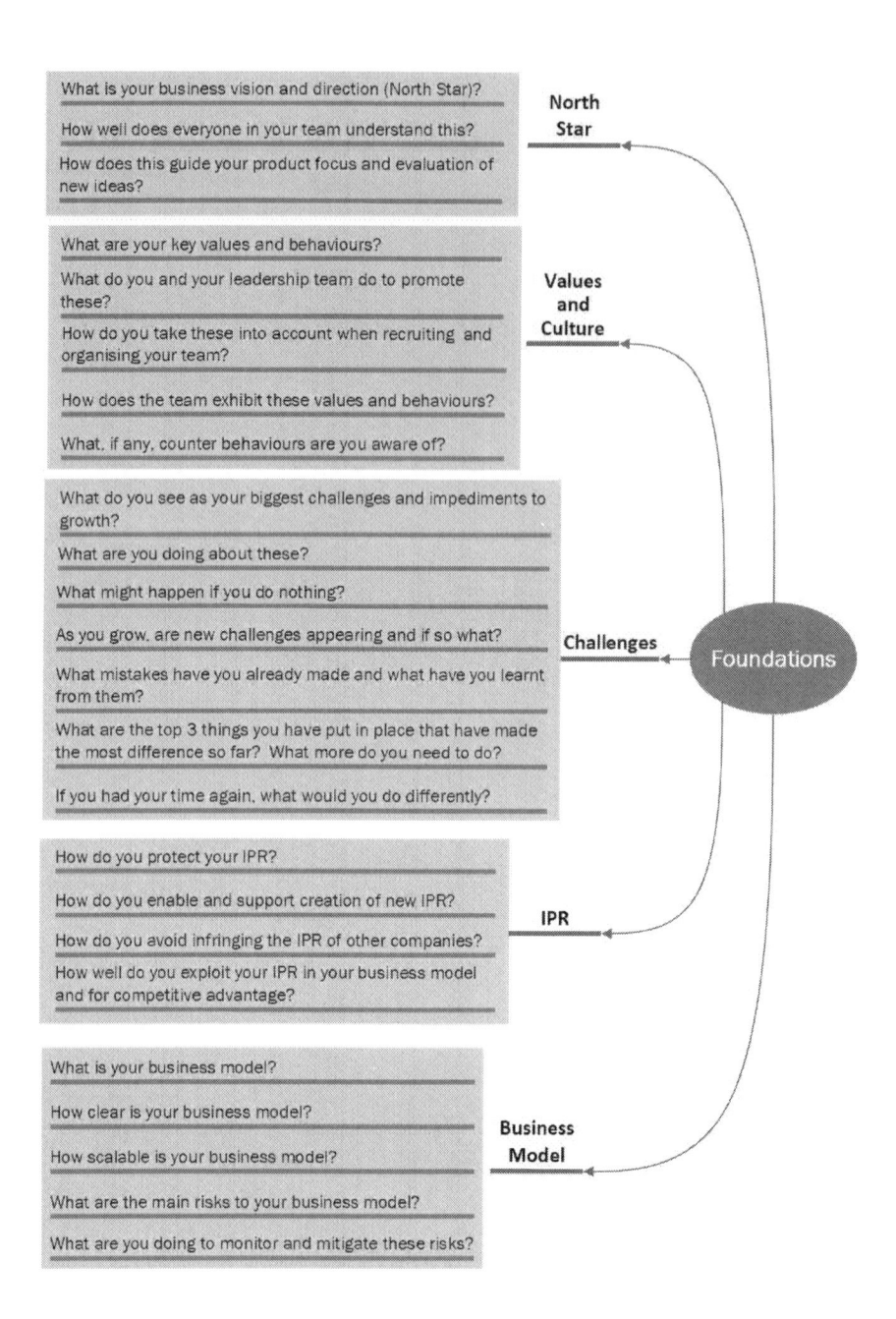

Foundations

North Star
- What is your business vision and direction (North Star)?
- How well does everyone in your team understand this?
- How does this guide your product focus and evaluation of new ideas?

Values and Culture
- What are your key values and behaviours?
- What do you and your leadership team do to promote these?
- How do you take these into account when recruiting and organising your team?
- How does the team exhibit these values and behaviours?
- What, if any, counter behaviours are you aware of?

Challenges
- What do you see as your biggest challenges and impediments to growth?
- What are you doing about these?
- What might happen if you do nothing?
- As you grow, are new challenges appearing and if so what?
- What mistakes have you already made and what have you learnt from them?
- What are the top 3 things you have put in place that have made the most difference so far? What more do you need to do?
- If you had your time again, what would you do differently?

IPR
- How do you protect your IPR?
- How do you enable and support creation of new IPR?
- How do you avoid infringing the IPR of other companies?
- How well do you exploit your IPR in your business model and for competitive advantage?

Business Model
- What is your business model?
- How clear is your business model?
- How scalable is your business model?
- What are the main risks to your business model?
- What are you doing to monitor and mitigate these risks?

Talent

What are your plans for growth?
What organisation will you need to achieve this and what additional talent is required?
How much do you consider developing existing team members before looking externally?
What values and attitudes do you seek in candidates and how do you verify these?
What are the key skills you need, including technical and people skills?
What do you do when there are insufficient candidates with the desired values and skills?
How important are analytical and learning skills to your team?
What do you look for in your leaders?
How do you evaluate these during the recruitment process?
How do you evaluate 'team fit' in the recruitment process?
What recruitment channels do you use? Have you considered any others including different locations and talent pools?
How do you differentiate yourself and attract the right talent to your business?
How do you share your business story, past, present and future?
How do you measure the success of your recruitment?
How quickly do new recruits typically start adding value?
How well do you retain staff?
As you have grown, how have your recruitment needs changed?
How do you expect these to change going forward?
How much do you consult your team on their ability to support new people?
How sustainable is the current workload of your team and how much capacity does it have for more work?
In what ways do you allow time for experimentation and play?
How do you take advantage of any new ideas that arise from this?
What evidence is there of continuous improvement in the team?
How much capacity has your workspace for growth?

Working Together

- What are the strengths and weaknesses of your current teams?
- How well are current team members suited to their roles?
- How do the individual, team and manager define these roles?
- How flexible is your team in terms or organising around member's individual strengths and weaknesses?
- Which areas could be improved by updated processes?
- How well have the current processes coped with growth so far?
- How might these be improved to support further growth?
- How do you evaluate new processes and who does this?
- When considering new ways of working, how much do your cultural foundations limit your options?
- What signs are there that silos are appearing?
- What indicators are there of miscommunication between individuals or teams?
- How do you evaluate team morale and what have you found?
- How good is team productivity?

Leadership

- What are the strengths and weaknesses of your leadership team?
- How open is the leadership team and how strong is the trust between leaders?
- How does the leadership team handle its workload and demands on its time?
- How much time do you and your leadership team spend firefighting?
- How much capacity do you have to steer the business towards high growth?
- How does what you do now compare to what you expected you would be doing when you started the business?
- How much do you and your leaders embody and exhibit the core company values and behaviours?
- How well do you and your leadership team provide and communicate a clear focus and vision to the rest of the business? How do you evaluate this?
- How well do you empower your teams to deliver? How well do you remove any impediments to this?
- What skills do you seek in your leaders? How much due diligence do you perform when hiring a new leader?
- How effective is the decision-making process in your leadership team? How might this be improved?
- How well do your functional leaders inspire, steer and grow their teams?
- What organisational silos are you aware of and what is the leadership team doing about these?
- How well does your leadership manage the challenges of success and failure?

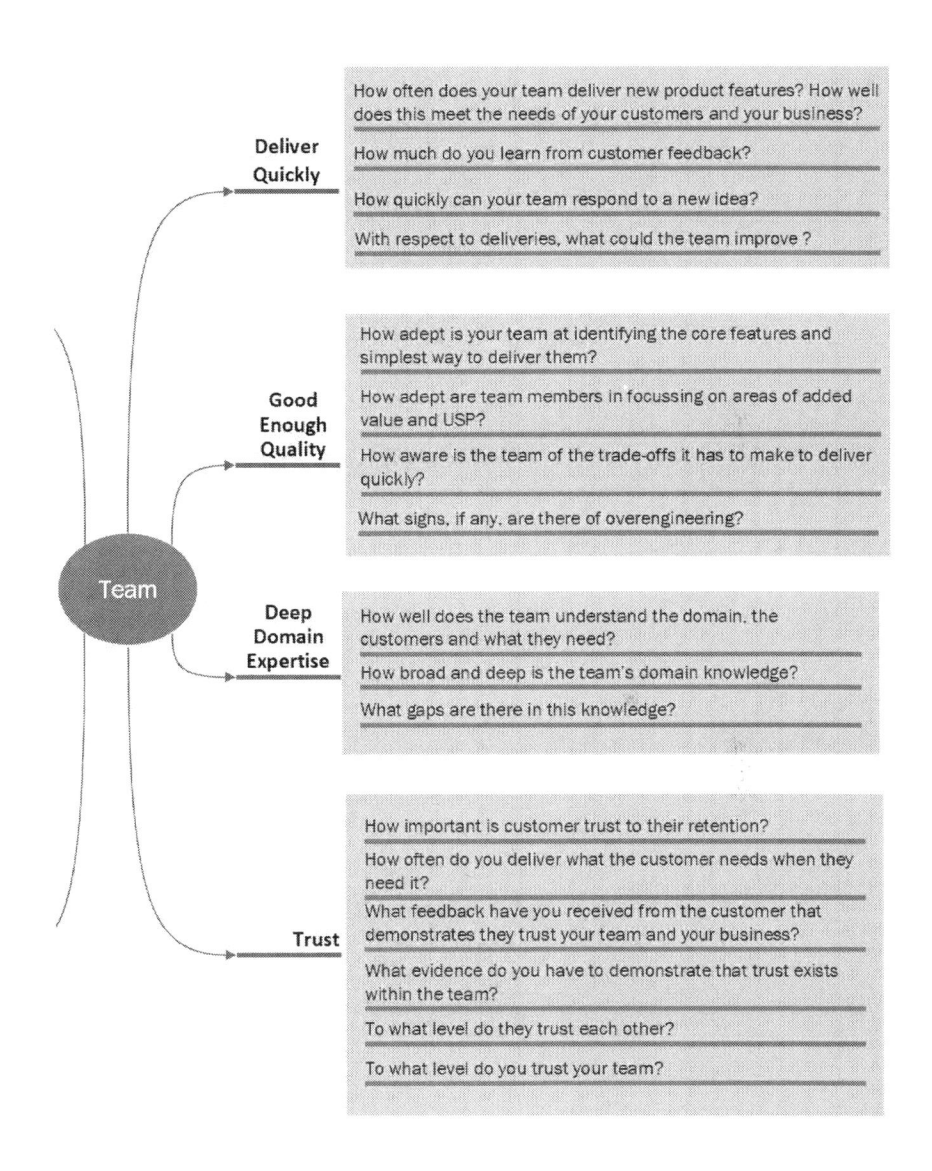

Team

Deliver Quickly
- How often does your team deliver new product features? How well does this meet the needs of your customers and your business?
- How much do you learn from customer feedback?
- How quickly can your team respond to a new idea?
- With respect to deliveries, what could the team improve?

Good Enough Quality
- How adept is your team at identifying the core features and simplest way to deliver them?
- How adept are team members in focussing on areas of added value and USP?
- How aware is the team of the trade-offs it has to make to deliver quickly?
- What signs, if any, are there of overengineering?

Deep Domain Expertise
- How well does the team understand the domain, the customers and what they need?
- How broad and deep is the team's domain knowledge?
- What gaps are there in this knowledge?

Trust
- How important is customer trust to their retention?
- How often do you deliver what the customer needs when they need it?
- What feedback have you received from the customer that demonstrates they trust your team and your business?
- What evidence do you have to demonstrate that trust exists within the team?
- To what level do they trust each other?
- To what level do you trust your team?

Product

Value
- What is the essential value of your product to your customers?
- How much do customers love what you provide?
- What critical problems does your product fix?
- How might this be enhanced? What might reduce the value to the customer?
- How focussed is your product on a particular market?
- How strong is your market share? How could this be improved?
- Where does your product sit on the horizontal-vertical market spectrum?
- How disruptive is your product?
- Who are your competitors?
- Where do they sit on the disruptive-incumbent spectrum?

Delivery
- How often do you deliver to, and engage with, customers?
- How well does your product deliver what the customers need, when they need it?
- How assured and consistent are your deliveries? How often do you deliver on time?
- How well does your product keep up with demand?

Focus
- How well does the product move you towards your vision?
- How clear is your focus on the most promising product features?
- How many ideas do you usually advance at one time?
- How has the increasing numbers of customers impacted your focus?
- How might you adapt your focus to meet the needs of rapidly increasing customer numbers?
- How much is progress impeded by your current resources?
- What opportunities do you have to increase your resources when required?
- How many different customer requests or ideas are you receiving and then progressing?
- Given your focus, how well do you deliver all the ideas you want to?

Pivot to Find the Right Product
- How much are you guided by your business vision?
- How close are you to finding the highest value product for customers?
- How will you know when you have found the right product? What do you evaluate to determine this?
- How good is your business at evaluating the need to pivot and then executing it? What impedes this?
- How good are you at spotting market shifts?

Growth

Retain Customers
- How well do you retain existing customers?
- How many strong, long-term customer relationships do you have?
- What proportion of your revenue comes from repeat business?
- How much do customers value your support services?

Win New Customers
- How does your product support the varying needs of your potential customer base?
- How efficient is this?
- What is your product strategy with respect to the core and custom modules?
- How much can customers or partners adapt your product?
- How coherent is your current product family?
- How well does your product meet the requirements of different geographic regions?

Engineer for Scale
- What opportunities have you seen for rapid growth? What signs of increasing demand are you seeing and can you meet it?
- How well does your product scale to meet these demands?
- How has your product been engineered to scale?
- How has your product been engineered to protect the customer from product or infrastructure failures? What more can be done to improve this?
- What is your customers' perception of the quality and reliability of your products?
- How do you plan for rapidly increasing customer loads? How do you forecast increasing customer loads?
- What are the current product limitations? Which must be addressed to enable continued growth?
- How prepared is your team to deliver a scalable, resilient service?
- What are the essential skills to provide this service? Are any of these missing or inadequate?
- How does your business vision guide the trade-offs required to scale your services or solutions?
- How well does your team keep abreast of the latest technologies and services that improve scalability and reliability?
- How well does your team understand the critical customer journeys through your services?
- How much does your team design for system failure?

Sell New Products
- How well do you identify new product opportunities with your customers?
- How do the new products complement existing ones?
- What pricing flexibility do you have across your full product range?
- How do you differentiate your product range from those of competitors?

Exploit market shifts
- What market shifts are you observing and which do you want to exploit?
- How ready are you to exploit these? Can you move fast enough?
- Are any market shifts a threat to your business? How significant are these threats?

Create Strategic Alliances
- Which businesses are potential partners who would increase your market reach?
- Which businesses might be potential acquisition targets and why?
- How good is the cultural fit between these businesses and yours?

Regular reviews for each of the 4 key stages, will ensure the whole organisation focusses on continuous improvements that lead to sustained growth. Not only that, reviews will help highlight emerging leaders within a team and give them visibility of wider roles.

This framework is intentionally simple. It allows you to focus on what matters and not be distracted by the means with which to achieve this.

For more information and resources, visit www.digitalhunters.co.uk.

2. LIFT OFF!

"I'll only be five minutes." I reassure Annie as I dash out of our taxi and into the foyer of my office building.

"Hello Mr. Ross, I haven't seen you for a while." I'm pleased to see Dennis with his broad smile again.

"You're looking very smart – been somewhere nice tonight?" he enquires.

"Tonight Dennis, I have been to a very special celebration."

"That's nice Mr. Ross. Good to let your hair down now and again."

"Indeed, it is Dennis, indeed it is. Must dash … got a meter running." I sprint to my office as he returns to his vacuum cleaner.

Placing the award on my desk, I pick up my laptop and head back to the taxi. I'd have liked to have said "Goodnight" to Dennis but the foyer is deserted.

Back in the taxi, Annie smiles and wearily leans her head on my shoulder. Tired but happy, I drift into my thoughts.

> *He's a good bloke Dennis and he's right, it is a long time since we last saw each other and yet in another way it seems like yesterday. I'll never forget his kind words. But more importantly, I'll never regret the next step I took straight afterwards.*

> *Once I started looking, it really didn't take long to find someone to help me think about the business and plan the way forward. Wow … what a difference that move made. I've got a trusted adviser now … a second pair of eyes on the whole picture. The great thing is, there's no agenda, no hidden motives. It's all about helping me succeed.*

I hear the taxi driver's voice. "We've cleared the roadworks now Sir, shouldn't be much longer." I nod back.

> *I think the main thing that initially stopped me looking for someone was fear of showing vulnerability. I've never found it a problem to talk about my strengths but it's the other side I needed to discuss if the business was ever to move on in the right direction. I don't feel so alone with it all now and I have certainly never felt judged, just understood. I feel much more confident leading the business.*

> *And how fantastic is the team! They're all motoring in the right direction now and we're focussing on what really matters. And, mercifully, I don't have to oversee everything personally anymore. It just shows what happens when you put the right people together.*

I glance at Annie, she's fast asleep.

> *Thankfully, Annie and I are on the same page now too. We're spending more time together and we've got some plans for our summer holiday. That all feels so different to how it was.*

I yawn, ready for bed but not in that exhausted and wired way I did before. I sleep much more soundly now knowing that most days, I've achieved so much.

> *How did I survive so long on such lousy sleep?*

"Which house is yours Sir?" I look out of the window. We're nearly home. "Third one on the left thanks." I reply.

> *Yes, things really are going how I intended when I first started the business. There's still much to be achieved and a great deal of hard work ahead, but I'm loving every minute of it ... well almost every minute.*

The business is really taking off. Customers love us and our products. More are knocking at the door. But we're keeping up and service levels are top notch.

We're in good shape. No ... we're in great shape!

I don't know exactly where this journey's going to end but I've mapped it out now and I can see the path we're going to follow. For sure, there'll be some twists and turns yet, but we can handle those.

I know we're creating something really special!

ABOUT THE AUTHOR

David Wicks is an entrepreneur, founder of Digital Hunters and TEDx speaker. He has 26 years' experience of software engineering, both in successful start-up companies and the leading-edge multi-nationals, News Corporation, Cisco and Sky Europe.

Throughout his extensive career in tech businesses, David has experienced both exciting highs and despairing uncertainties. With deep domain knowledge, he understands closely, the rollercoaster nature of the tech world.

David works with individuals, teams and whole organisations. He has a passion that empowers others, helps them build a company to be proud of, create the wealth they deserve and leave an enduring legacy.

Learn more at www.digitalhunters.co.uk.

DISCLAIMER

On the Fast 50:

The Deloitte UK Technology Fast 50 is a list of the 50 fastest growing UK-based technology companies, based on revenue growth over the last four years. The UK Fast 50 is part of an international program run by Deloitte. Deloitte does not own or control or have any affiliation with the companies which form part of the UK Fast 50. The list is compiled on the basis of the financial information provided by the companies. Technology companies can be nominated for the awards if certain eligibility criteria relating to period of operation, ownership and revenue are met. In nominating a company for consideration, details of the company's revenue and copies of signed, audited and unabbreviated accounts must be provided. The assessment of the fastest growing companies is calculated using this information. A company's ranking and inclusion on the list is a factual assessment based on growth figures and does not incorporate an assessment of the quality of the services offered by the company.

On the book's content:

Please note that David Wicks and Horndale Solutions Limited are entirely independent of Deloitte. Save for the foreword, which has been written by David Cobb (Deloitte Partner), Deloitte has not contributed to the content of this publication. Deloitte accepts no liability for any loss occasioned to any person acting or refraining from acting as a result of any material in this publication. In this publication, references to Deloitte are references to Deloitte LLP. Deloitte LLP is a limited liability partnership registered in England and Wales with registered number OC303675 and its registered office at 2 New Street Square, London EC4A 3BZ, United Kingdom. Deloitte LLP is the United Kingdom affiliate of Deloitte NWE LLP, a member firm of Deloitte Touche Tohmatsu Limited, a UK private company limited by guarantee ("DTTL"). DTTL and each of its member firms are legally separate and independent entities. DTTL and Deloitte NWE LLP do not provide services to clients.

REFERENCES

[1] Ries, E 2011, *The Lean Startup*, Portfolio Penguin, London.

[2] Waitley, D 2009, *Psychology of Success*, McGraw-Hill Higher Education, Burr Ridge.

[3] RSA Insurance Group 2014, 'Growing Pains: Majority of SMES Don't Survive Five Years', *RSA Insurance Group News*, accessed 6 June 2018, <https://www.rsagroup.com/news/press-releases/2014/growing-pains-majority-of-smes-dont-survive-five-years/>.

[4] RSA Insurance Group 2014, 'Growing Pains: How the UK became a nation of "micropreneurs" ', accessed 7 June 2018, <https://www.rsagroup.com/media/1737/growing-pains-how-the-uk-became-a-nation-of.pdf>.

[5] Palmer, J 2018, 'UK corporate financial health deteriorates since Article 50 was triggered', *Begbies Traynor Business Health Statistics*, accessed 6 June 2018, <https://www.begbies-traynorgroup.com/news/business-health-statistics/uk-corporate-financial-health-deteriorates-since-article-50-was-triggered>.

[6] Gompers, P, Kovner, A, Lerner, J, Scharfstein, D 2008, 'Performance Persistence in Entrepreneurship', *Harvard Business School Working Paper*, accessed 6 June 2018, <https://www.hbs.edu/faculty/Publication%20Files/09-028.pdf>.

[7] Oliva, R, Sterman, J, Giese, M 2003, 'Limits to Growth in the New Economy: Exploring the 'Get Big Fast' Strategy in e-commerce', *System Dynamics Review* 19(2):83-117, accessed 6 June 2018, <http://iops.tamu.edu/faculty/roliva/research/dotcom/>.

[8] Marmer, M, Herrmann, B, Dogrultan, E, Berman, R 2011, 'Startup Genome Report Extra on Premature Scaling: A deep dive into why most high growth startups fail', *Startup Genome Report*: premature scaling, accessed 6 June 2018,

<http://gallery.mailchimp.com/8c534f3b5ad611c0ff8aeccd5/files/Startup_Genome_Report_Extra_Premature_Scaling_version_2.1.pdf>.

[9] Bensinger, G 2015, 'Rebuilding History's Biggest Dot-Com Bust: Online-Grocery Firm Instacart Farms Out Jobs and Food, Hoping to Make It Where Webvan Failed', *The Wall Street Journal*, accessed 6 June 2018, <https://www.wsj.com/articles/rebuilding-historys-biggest-dot-come-bust-1421111794>.

[10] Schneider, W 1994, *The Re-engineering Alternative: A Plan for making your current culture work,* McGraw-Hill, New York.

[11] Johnson, R, Fraser, J 2010, 'EventVue post-mortem', *Facebook Notes EventVue*, accessed 6 June 2018, <https://www.facebook.com/notes/eventvue/eventvue-post-mortem/470086850385>.

[12] Sivers, D 2012, ' "Unlearning": Everything is my fault', *Derek Sivers Blog*, accessed 6 June 2018, <https://sivers.org/my-fault>.

[13] Hedlund, Marc 2010, 'Why Wesabe Lost to Mint', *Marc Hedlund's Blog*, accessed 6 June 2018, <http://blog.precipice.org/why-wesabe-lost-to-mint/>.

[14] Osterwalder, A, Pigneur, Y 2010, *Business Model Generation: A Handbook for Visionaries, Game Changers, and Challengers,* John Wiley & Sons, Hoboken.

[15] Weill, P, Malone, T, D'Urso, V, Herman, G, Woerner, S 2004, 'Do Some Business Models Perform Better than Others? A Study of the 1000 Largest US Firms', *Sloan School of Management Massachusetts Institute of Technology*, MIT Center for Coordination Science Working Paper No. 226, accessed 6 June 2018, <http://ccs.mit.edu/papers/pdf/wp226.pdf>.

[16] Maurya, A 2010, 'How to Document Your Business Model On 1 Page', *Ash Maurya Blog: Love the Problem*, accessed 6 June 2018, < https://blog.leanstack.com/how-to-document-your-business-model-on-1-page-a6c91ab73efd>.

[17] Maurya, A 2012, *Running Lean: Iterate from Plan A to a Plan That Works*, O'Reilly Media, Sebastopol.

[18] Berry, T 2015, *Lean Business Planning: Get What You Want From Your Business*, Motivational Press, Carlsbad.

[19] Weinberg, G 1992, *Quality Software Management Volume 1: Systems Thinking*, Dorset House Publishing, New York.

[20] Spotify Training & Development 2014, 'Spotify Engineering Culture - part 1', accessed 6 June 2018, <https://vimeo.com/85490944>.

[21] Wicks, D 2017, 'The Unicorn and Phoenix – Lessons in Failure from VE Interactive', LinkedIn Article, accessed 6 June 2018, <https://www.linkedin.com/pulse/unicorn-phoenix-lessons-failure-from-ve-interactive-david-wicks/ >.

[22] Highsmith, J 2002, *Agile Software Development Ecosystems*, Pearson Education, Boston.

[23] Beck, K et al. 2001, 'The Manifesto for Agile Software Development', accessed 6 June 2018, <http://agilemanifesto.org/>.

[24] Poland, S 2011, 'The little startup that couldn't (a postmortem of MyFavorites)', *Steve Poland Analysis Blog*, accessed 6 June 2018, <http://www.stevepoland.com/the-little-startup-that-couldnt-a-postmortem-of-myfavorites/>.

[25] Biggar, P 2010, 'Why we shut NewsTilt down', *Paul Biggar Blog - Medium*, accessed 6 June 2018, <https://medium.com/@paulbiggar/why-we-shut-newstilt-down-5aba6a11136f>.

[26] Lencioni , P 2002, *The Five Dysfunctions of a Team: A Leadership Fable*, Jossey-Bass, San Francisco.

[27] Christensen, C 2013, *The Innovator's Dilemma: When New Technologies Cause Great Firms to Fail (Management of Innovation and Change)*, Harvard Business Review Press, Watertown.

[28] Darshan, B 2016, 'What is the main reason of the downfall of blackberry company?', *Quora*, accessed 6 June 2018, <https://www.quora.com/What-is-the-main-reason-of-the-downfall-of-blackberry-company>.

[29] Nygard, M 2007, *Release It! Design and Deploy Production-Ready Software*, The Pragmatic Bookshelf, Dallas,

[30] Anthony, S 2016, 'Kodak's Downfall Wasn't About Technology', *Harvard Business Review*, accessed 6 June 2018, < https://hbr.org/2016/07/kodaks-downfall-wasnt-about-technology>.

[31] Investopedia, '5 Biggest Acquisition Failures Of All Time', accessed 6 June 2018, <https://www.investopedia.com/slide-show/biggest-acquisition-failures/>.

Printed in Poland
by Amazon Fulfillment
Poland Sp. z o.o., Wrocław